EPHRAIM

Chosen of
the Lord

R. Wayne Shute
Monte S. Nyman
Randy L. Bott

Millennial Press
Salt Lake City, Utah

Millennial Press, Inc.
11968 South Doves Landing Drive
Riverton, Utah 84065

Publisher's Cataloging-in-Publication
(Provided by Quality Books, Inc.)

Shute, R. Wayne.
    Ephraim, chosen of the Lord : what it means
to be of the tribe of Ephraim / R. Wayne Shute,
Monte S. Nyman, Randy L. Bott. -- 1st ed.
    p. cm.
    Includes bibliographical references and
index.
  LCCN: 98-68613
  ISBN: 0-9660231-3-7

  1. Church of Jesus Christ of Latter-day
Saints--Doctrines. 2. Twelve tribes of Israel.
3. Ephraim (Tribe of Israel) I. Nyman, Monte
S. II. Bott, Randy L., 1945- III. Title.

BX8643.L66S48 1999   289.3'32
           QBI98-1770

05 04 03 02   10 9 8 7 6 5 4 3

Table of Contents

Introduction 1

Chapter 1: Ephraim, Chosen Before Thou Wast Born 7

Chapter 2: Biblical Ephraim, Son of Joseph 17

Chapter 3: The Land Given to Ephraim 25

Chapter 4: Ephraim and the Judgments of God. 29

Chapter 5: Biblical Prophecies Concerning the
Gathering of Ephraim 37

Chapter 6: Ephraim in The Book of Mormon 51

Chapter 7: Ephraim in the Doctrine and Covenants 59

Chapter 8: Ephraim to be Opposed in the Latter-days 69

Chapter 9: Go Forth My Sons [Ephraim] and Find the
Lost Sheep of the House of Israel 77

Chapter 10: Ephraim and Temple Work 85

Chapter 11: Ephraim and the Perfecting of the Saints. 97

Appendix 1: "The Second Gathering of the Literal Seed"
adapted from a paper presented at The Sperry Symposium
October 1988 by Monte S. Nyman who, at the time,
was Associate Dean of Religious Education,
Brigham Young University. 111

Bibliography 120

Appendix 2: A dramatic poem written for the April 1930
General Conference of The Church of Jesus Christ of
Latter-day Saints by Orson F. Whitney, "The Lifted Ensign—
A Call to Israel" 121

Introduction

Most Latter-day Saints are familiar with the name Ephraim, yet most people seem to know little about him and his work, especially pertaining to his responsibilities in these latter-days. In truth, most of us associate the name of Ephraim with our patriarchal blessings wherein there is a declaration something like the following, "Brother or Sister Jones, thou art of Ephraim through the loins of Joseph!" In these and words similar to them is declared our lineage and establishes us as part of the chosen tribe of Ephraim within the House of Israel.

No doubt we have all pondered and weighed in a general way the significance of our patriarchal blessings and no doubt some of us have raised questions about the meaning of our declared lineage. In the case of Ephraim, "What does it mean to be of this tribe?" "Are we talking here of the literal blood of Ephraim?" "Does it really matter, in the great scheme of things, what tribe of Israel we belong to?" And, of great importance to someone not of the tribe of Ephraim, "What will happen to me? Will I have a lesser blessing?" We have attempted in this book to answer these and other questions pertaining to the lineage of Ephraim.

We have organized the book into eleven chapters. We begin by addressing the sensitive issues surrounding the favored position of Ephraim in these last days particularly regarding Ephraim's responsibilities and blessings; we then discuss Ephraim in the context of biblical history and setting; we then move from the Bible to a discussion of references in The Book of Mormon and the Doctrine and Covenants and attempt to give a "restored" look at Ephraim. We follow these chapters with a discussion of the adversary's evil effort in trying to thwart the work of Ephraim; and then follow this with three chapters: one on the missionary responsibility of Ephraim, the next on Ephraim and temple work, and the third constitutes a discussion of the work of Ephraim in perfecting the Saints. In addition, we have included in the Appendix two documents which we think will be of interest. The first is an adaptation of a paper which Monte S. Nyman presented at BYU in October 1988 entitled, "The Second Gathering of the Literal Seed." Finally, we present, in full, a dramatic poem about the work of Ephraim in the last days written by Orson F. Whitney which he presented in the April 1930 General Conference of the Church.

Ephraim's Responsibility and Blessing

This is a book written from a particular point of view pertaining to the lineage of Joseph. We humbly and modestly submit that, according to this point of view, Ephraim and his fellows have been **elected** to perform a special responsibility in these last days prior to the coming of our Lord and Savior, Jesus Christ. And we humbly submit also that if Ephraimites fulfill this responsibility which has been placed upon them, they may expect special, even eternal blessings.

Of the responsibility, Hyrum G. Smith said,

> I pray that the Lord will continue to be mindful of us that we may be more loyal in the future than we have been in the past, loyal to our callings and to our responsibilities; ...We are only a few in number compared to the great host in the world, and we must remember and know that where the Lord requires responsibility, he expects us to be loyal and true to it. Therefore, the responsibility is upon our shoulders as gathered Ephraim, living here in the land of Ephraim, in the tops of the mountains, in the midst of the everlasting hills, where the Lord has selected a gathering place and named it through the mouths of his holy prophets, both ancient and modern...here it [our responsibility] will be required at our hands, not only by our words but by our every day conduct.[1]

Melvin J. Ballard has added to the weight of this enormous responsibility placed upon the heads of latter-day Ephraimites. He said,

> God bless us that we shall treasure our heritage, that we shall recognize that we are to do an unusual thing. We are not called to be imitators, we are called to be exemplars to the world, a light that shall shine until the day will come when from the east to the west, the north to the south, they will come, not to look upon our lands nor our fields nor our factories, but to learn of our ways that they

---

[1] Smith, Hyrum G. General Conference Address, April 1923

may walk in our paths, and thereby find peace, preservation and salvation now and eternally.[2]

And Orson F. Whitney said about our responsibility,

> In preaching the gospel to the world and gathering Israel from the nations, the Latter-day Saints—children of Ephraim—are helping to fulfill the covenant made by Jehovah with Abraham, Isaac and Jacob: "In thee and in thy seed shall all the nations of the earth be blessed."[3]

In addition to modern prophets describing the responsibilities of Ephraim, ancient prophets as well foretold the work required at the hand of Ephraim in the last days. Said Jeremiah,

> For there shall be a day, that the watchmen upon the Mount Ephraim shall cry, Arise ye, and let us go up to Zion unto the Lord our God. For thus saith the Lord; Sing with gladness for Jacob, and shout among the chief of the nations: publish ye, praise ye, and say, O Lord, save thy people, the remnant of Israel.
>
> Behold, I will bring them from the north country, and gather them from the coasts of the earth, and with them the blind and the lame, the woman with child and her that travaileth with child together: a great company shall return thither.
>
> They shall come with weeping, and with supplications, will I lead them: I will cause them to walk by the rivers of waters in a straight way, wherein they shall not stumble: for I am a father to Israel, and Ephraim is my firstborn (Jeremiah 31: 6-9).

The tribe of Ephraim has a monumental mission to perform mainly because of Ephraim's birthright in Israel. "The Gospel is being preached by Ephraim to the nations...for he it is who is to prepare the way for the other tribes of Israel."[4]

When successful in this responsibility of preaching the Gospel to the world and doing all else that Ephraim is commanded to do, great blessings will be poured out. Among other things, the lost tribes of Israel

---

2 Ballard, Melvin J. General Conference Address, October 1927

3 Whitney, Orson, F. General Conference Address, April, 1928

4 Smith, Joseph Fielding The Way to Perfection, Chapter 18.

...shall bring forth their rich treasures unto the children of Ephraim, my servants.

And there shall they fall down and be crowned with glory, even in Zion, by the hands of the servants of the Lord, even the children of Ephraim.

And they shall be filled with songs of everlasting joy.

Behold, this is the blessing of the everlasting God upon the tribes of Israel, and the richer blessing upon the head of Ephraim and his fellows (D&C 133: 30, 32-34).

Ephraim, Towering Amid the Tents of Israel

In the April 1930 General Conference of the Church, Elder Orson F. Whitney was invited by President Heber J. Grant to read a dramatic poem, **The Lifted Ensign—A Call to Israel** [5] that he (Elder Whitney) had written "especially for this occasion." The poem is a cry, even a charge unto Ephraim to fulfill the responsibility that has been placed upon him and his fellows by the Lord to gather in the remnant of the House of Israel, including those who are of the House of Judah. The poem, which features reading parts for Elias, Ephraim and Judah, among other things expresses much of what we believe about the important work of Ephraim and sets the stage for what we have said in this book.

In answering the call from Elias to lead out in the gathering of Israel, Ephraim says,

I hear thee, and with joy I answer thee:
"Twas mine to welcome the return of Truth,
Of old from Error's wide domain withdrawn;
Mine to unshroud the buried mystery
Of mighty nations, whispering from the dust;
Mind to unfurl the Ensign, and to sound
O'er sea and land the tidings wonderful;
Flooding the world with truth and righteousness,
Thrusting the sickle in the golden grain,
Reaping a ripened field, and garnering
The earliest sheaves of Israel's harvest home.

---

[5] The dramatic poem by Elder Whitney entitled **The Lifted Ensign—A Call to Israel** is quoted in its entirety in Appendix Two.

4

I've toiled and wept and bled to bring once more
The fulness of Christ's Message unto men;
To build redemptive Temples, that the dead,
Obedient to law in spirit realms,
Might with the living share in joys divine,
More wouldst thou hear"—
There's more I fain would tell.

Elias urges Ephraim to "tell on! tell on!" Ephraim then describes the difficulty of the task given him. But, undaunted, he faces the task with courage and determination. He tells on,

Expelled by tyranny from Freedom's ground,
I tracked the lone untrodden wilderness.
Here 'neath my virile touch, once barren wilds
Now sing for joy and bloom delightsomely,
I've planted Zion's outposts, firm and strong,
Rock-fortressed by the everlasting hills,
Where Faith expectantly doth bide the hour
When Zion's self from Eden's soil shall rise,
Thrilled by the glad acclaim: "The Bridegroom comes!"
Nor ally my ministries on Western shores,
Nor all my sympathies with next of kin.
Have I not stood on ancient Olivet,
And offered prayer to heaven for Judah's weal?
Have I not combed the universe and drawn
The choice of nations to this favored land,
Where homing tribes shall shout to trembling hills,
And lift hosannas to the listening skies
That light the towers of New Jerusalem?
By these and kindred works my faith is shown.
Thus I have answered to the Shepherd's call.

We have been greatly sobered by the work accomplished through the efforts of many faithful Latter-day Saints—both those who worked with great faith in the early years of the Church and those in recent years, those who are now going forth to build the Kingdom of God on earth with faith and testimony. These are of Ephraim, bold and confident.

To this great work we are personally committed and hope, in our small way, this book will help us all understand more fully who we are and what we should be about, as a favored people, in these last days.

CHAPTER 1

Ephraim
Chosen Before Thou Wast Born

That there is great confusion in the world today, cannot be denied. Indeed, the Prophet Joseph Smith was told that the world was "under the most damning hand of murder, tyranny, and oppression" and that this damning hand was

> upheld by the influence of that spirit which hath so strongly riveted the creeds of the fathers, who have inherited lies, upon the hearts of the children, **and filled the world with confusion** (our emphasis), and has been growing stronger and stronger, and is now the very mainspring of all corruption, and the whole earth groans under the weight of its iniquity. (D&C 123:7)

Indeed, confusion reigns. Isaiah warned that in our day, "their works are in the dark." And, yet, those who are in the dark confuse things by saying, "Surely, your turning of things **upside down** shall be esteemed as the potter's clay." But, predicted Isaiah, the Lord knows "all their works. For shall the work say of him that made it, he made me not? Or shall the thing framed say of him that framed it, he had no understanding?" (2 Nephi 27:27)

Of all the confusion that does reign today, the one pertaining to the nature of man and his relationship with God is most pronounced. We speak particularly about the idea of a "chosen" or a "favored" people. For most people caught up in the political correctness of our day, however, this is an abhorrent idea. But we say, that if we are sufficiently humble to learn from the scriptures and modern prophets, we will be able to bring "to light all the hidden things" (D&C 123:13) so that we will know who we are and what earth life is all about—that God's plan is clear and equitable, even though some are chosen or favored.

Noble and Great Ones

So successful has the Adversary been in confusing the world that most of the churches of this day deny that man existed before he was born. If one looks at the totality of life as beginning at birth and ending with death, it is easy to look heavenward and accuse God of being partial or unfair. But life did not begin at birth for any one or anything on earth (Moses 3: 5-7). Neither did our progression towards perfection begin at birth. Neither did the development of our personalities, character, or strengths and weaknesses begin at birth. In fact, the Lord made it perfectly clear to father Abraham that many had distinguished themselves as "noble and great" before ever being born on this earth.

> Now the Lord had shown unto me, Abraham, the intelligences that were organized before the world was; and among all these there were many of the noble and great ones;
>
> And God saw these souls that they were good, and he stood in the midst of them, and he said: These I will make my rulers; for he stood among those that were spirits, and he saw that they were good; and he said unto me: Abraham, thou art one of them; thou wast chosen before thou wast born (Abraham 3: 22-23).

Speaking about these "noble and great ones," Erastus Snow gave the following insight about the nature of being a chosen spirit.

> For he has had his eye upon the chosen spirits that have come upon the earth in the various ages from the beginning of the world up to this time; and as he said to Abraham, speaking of the multitudes of spirits that were shown unto him in heavenly vision, you see that some are more noble than others? Yes. Then you may know there were some others still more noble than they; and he speaks in the same manner of the multitude of the heavenly bodies; and said he to Abraham, thou art one of those noble ones whom I have chosen to be my rulers. The Lord has sent those noble spirits into the world to perform a special work, and appointed their times; and they have always fulfilled the mission given them, and their future glory and exaltation is secured unto them; and that is what I understand by the doctrine of election spoken of by the Apostle Paul and other sacred writers: "For whom he did foreknow, he also did predestinate to be conformed to the image of His Son, that he might be the first-born

among many brethren." Such were called and chosen and elected of God to perform a certain work at a certain time of the world's history and in due time he fitted them for that work... And so he elected the seed of Ephraim to be that peculiar people I have referred to, that holy nation, a kingdom of Priests, a people to receive the covenants and oracles, and to be witnesses to certain nations of the God of Israel.[6]

So who are the "noble and great ones" so highly spoken of in holy writ? Let us turn to the scriptures and the modern day leaders for much needed insight. While the "politically correct" thinkers of the world condemn the divine practice of choosing and foreordaining certain individuals and peoples for specific tasks and positions in mortality, President Joseph Fielding Smith challenged their right to dictate to God whom He would choose.

Our history of those events informs us that Jacob was called before he was born to inherit these blessings. Then they were given him by the highest Authority, and who dare question the right of that Authority to bestow the blessings?[7]

The Lord has not revealed to mankind the duration of the time we spent in pre-mortal life. The extent of the progress that was made has also, in His wisdom, been kept from us. However, He has revealed the formula He used when he preplanned the sequencing, the duration, the configuration, the assignments, and the promised inheritances of His children upon the earth. He revealed to Moses:

When the most High divided to the nations their inheritance, when he separated the sons of Adam, he set the bounds of the people according to the number of the children of Israel. For the LORD'S portion is his people; Jacob is the lot of his inheritance (Deuteronomy 32: 8-9).

Imagine, the entire population of the earth was and continues to be placed on earth according to the numbers of the children of Israel! Does that mean that the omniscient mind of God contemplated the mortal experience of each of His spirit children? Let the scriptures speak for themselves. "For whom he did foreknow, he also did predestinate to be

---

[6] Erastus Snow, <u>Journal of Discourses</u>, Vol. 23, p. 184 - p. 185, May 6, 1982
[7] Joseph Fielding Smith Jr., <u>The Way to Perfection</u>, p. 117

conformed to the image of his Son, that he might be the firstborn among many brethren." (Romans 8: 29)

One might ask: "Who of all the spirit sons and daughters of God did He not know? Since the Lord's stated objective is to help His children gain eternal life[8], it stands to reason that the omniscient, omnipotent Father would place each child in a position which: 1) he or she had earned, and 2) which, if taken full advantage of, would enhance their progressions towards exaltation faster than any other condition. The Lord enlarges our understanding of the extent of this pre-earth choosing by revealing through the Apostle Paul, "And hath made of one blood all nations of men for to dwell on all the face of the earth, and hath determined the times before appointed, and the bounds of their habitation." (Acts 17: 26)

A Chosen People

Elaborating on the idea of being chosen for a particular time and for a particular reason, a modern apostle has said,

> I was thrilled not long ago when I read an article appearing in one of our national magazines. The author was discussing the question: "Are the Jews the Chosen People of God?" He denied them the right to claim for themselves and their posterity all the blessings pronounced upon all the sons of Jacob, but limited their blessings to their own particular line—the tribe of Judah. After tracing the history of the Jews and the several tribes of Israel the author concludes: "If we could find in the earth somewhere today the descendants of Joseph, we would find the chosen people of God," because the blessings of Joseph were so much greater than the blessings of his brethren that you will recall they despised him and were jealous of his blessings, and sold him into Egypt; but the Lord was with him and raised him up and made him mighty to become the deliverer of his father's household." I say, when I read that statement my soul thrilled with a new sensation of gratitude to God that I live to see the day when Joseph's children are being gathered again, and realize that the Latter-day Saints are of Joseph, children of his favored son, Ephraim, gathered "one of a city and two of a family," a few from the midst of the nations of the earth, whither they have been scattered, and brought to the land of Zion. The Lord has

---

[8] See Moses 1:39

selected and picked them. They were chosen spirits before they were born. He knew them in the spirit world. He held them in reserve to come forth at the right time.[9]

One might question the reasons why the Almighty would choose one portion of His family over another. He has revealed, however, some of the reasons for designating a chosen people as noted in the following,

> The reasons for the choosing of a special nation to bear the Priesthood and be favored with the oracles of truth are many. It is both consistent and reasonable for the Lord to call such people and bestow upon them special favors, when all the rest of mankind rejected the word. Through this covenant people the Lord reserved the right to send into the world a chosen lineage of faithful spirits who were entitled to special favors based on pre-mortal obedience. Moreover, the choosing of a special race, and the conferring upon it of peculiar covenants and obligations, which other nations would not keep, had the effect of segregating this race from other races.[10]

The idea of designating a favored people has been a practice employed by the Almighty from the foundation of this earth, not to suppress or inhibit the progress of His children, but to actually enhance their progress. It is one thing to be chosen, however, it is quite another to accept the responsibility associated with that choosing. President Wilford Woodruff taught,

> We are the seed of Ephraim, and of Abraham, and of Joseph, who was sold into Egypt, and these are the instruments that God has kept in the spirit world to come forth in these latter days to take hold of this kingdom and build it up.[11]

Speaking prophetically, yet modestly, the Prophet Joseph Smith has informed us of the nature of our callings before we ever came to this earth. He said,

> Every man who has a calling to minister to the inhabitants of the world was ordained to that very purpose in the Grand Council of heaven before this world was. I suppose I was ordained to this very office in

---

[9] Melvin J. Ballard, Conference Report, October 1924, p. 28

[10] Joseph Fielding Smith Jr., The Way to Perfection, p. 129-130

[11] Wilford Woodruff, Journal of Discourses 22:233, June 26, 1881

that Grand Council. It is the testimony that I want that I am God's servant, and this people His people. The ancient prophets declared that in the last days the God of heaven should set up a kingdom which should never be destroyed, nor left to other people; and the very time that was calculated on, this people were struggling to bring it out.[12]

Using current population statistics, how likely is it that any given baby would be born a Latter-day Saint, the vast majority of whom are of the tribe of Ephraim? There are approximately ten million Latter-day Saints in the world with approximately five and a half billion people. That would mean that for every 550 babies born on the earth, only one is a Latter-day Saint! We don't think this is by chance. In fact, Orson F. Whitney forcefully reminded us of our heritage and our duty.

They were chosen in the heavens, before they came in the flesh, and were sent forth from the presence of God with a mission. We who call ourselves Latter-day Saints are a branch of the house of Israel, gathered out from among the Gentiles; we are a portion of that martyred nation, chosen of God and sent upon earth to suffer and endure for His sake and for the sake of all mankind; to bear the oracles of God, and be His representatives in the midst of the human race. Read what Moses says in the eighth verse of the 32nd chapter of Deuteronomy, if you doubt that Israel had an existence before the earthly days of Father Abraham...What does this mean, If not that Israel was a pro-existent race, ordained before the world was to perform the great and important mission that has rested upon them all down the ages, and a portion of which is now being performed by the Latter-day Saints, the gathered children of Ephraim.[13]

A Chosen People, A Heavy Task

How could Ephraim possibly fulfill his foreordained task of preparing the entire world for the Second Coming of Christ? There are so many nations which have not yet been granted the fulness of the gospel that one might despair at the enormity of our assigned task. Yet Joseph Fielding Smith, in answering the probing question of a missionary, gave additional insight:

---

[12] Teachings of the Prophet Joseph Smith, Section Six 1843-44 p. 365
[13] Orson F. Whitney, Conference Report, October 1905, p. 91

Question: "My companion and I were discussing the lineage of the Israelites. I am a full blood Chinese, and have thought much of my lineage as mentioned in my patriarchal blessing. When I told my companion that my blessing said 'You are of the lineage of Abraham, Isaac, Jacob, and Ephraim,' he commented that I must not be pure Chinese. Since he has made such a statement, I have thought much about what is mentioned in the blessing. I will be grateful if you will inform me as to the relationship between races: Chinese, French, German, and others. I am particularly interested in this because I interpret the lineage literally and not as an adoption... [Part of President Smith's answer was as follows] "All of this [scattering of Israel among the nations of the world] was to come on Israel as a punishment for their wickedness. However, the Lord never punishes his people without turning that punishment into some blessing in the end. The scattering of Israel became a blessing to the Gentile peoples among whom they were dispersed, for the Israelites mixed with the people thus bringing the Gentiles into the benefits of the blessings that had been promised to Abraham and his seed after him. Nearly all of the Latter-day Saints are of Gentile ancestry as well as being of the house of Israel."[14]

It is no mistake that we are here now. The task we have been Divinely given is difficult but not impossible. The sons and daughters of God who are being sent to earth at this time have had years of preparation for the task they are assigned. The opposition is greater than at any time during the long and tumultuous history of this earth. Yet President Ezra Taft Benson gave us this expansive vision,

For nearly six thousand years, God has held you in reserve to make your appearance in the final days before the Second Coming of the Lord... While our generation will be comparable in wickedness to the days of Noah, when the Lord cleansed the earth by flood, there is a major difference this time. It is that God has saved for the final inning some of his strongest children, who will help bear off the Kingdom triumphantly. And that is where you come in, for you are the generation that must be prepared to meet your God.

All through the ages the prophets have looked down through the corridors of time to our day. Billions of the deceased and those yet

---

[14] Joseph Fielding Smith, <u>Answers to Gospel Questions</u>, Vol. 4, p. 36, 38

to be born have their eyes on us. Make no mistake about it—you are a marked generation. There has never been more expected of the faithful in such a short period of time as there is of us. Never before on the face of this earth have the forces of evil and the forces of good been as well organized. Now is the great day of the devil's power, with the greatest mass murderers of all time living among us. But now is also the great day of the Lord's power, with the greatest number ever of priesthood holders on the earth. And the showdown is fast approaching.[15]

Since the veil of forgetfulness has been dropped over the memory of mankind, it was deemed necessary by the Almighty to provide a way of giving us a glimpse of where we came from, what is expected of us, and the attendant blessings (both temporal and spiritual) which we are heir to. Orson Pratt enlightens us as to how the Lord intended to reveal our true identity:

Being prophets, the Lord inspired them to know and understand the future, to know what he intended to perform and accomplish on the earth. They understood by the spirit of prophecy the blessings that would come upon the righteous and the curses that would come upon the wicked. They understood that the Lord would bestow blessings bountifully upon those who would serve him and keep his commandments. Hence they predicted blessings upon them, not only of a spiritual nature but of a temporal nature, among which farms were given to them, kingdoms, thrones, and a great variety of blessings of a temporal nature were oftentimes conferred by the spirit of prophecy upon the descendants of those whom the Lord delighted in.[16]

Summary

Summarizing what the scriptures and the latter-day prophets have said, we conclude that people are not born on to the earth by accident. The blessings received here are predicated on countless years of pre-mortal life. According to strengths and talents developed in the pre-mortal existence, and at the direction of the omniscient Father, all of His

---

[15] Ezra Taft Benson "In His Steps," in <u>Speeches of the Year</u>, 1979 Provo: BYU Press, 1980, pg. 59

[16] <u>Journal of Discourses</u>, Vol. 14, p. 7 - p. 8, Orson Pratt, February 19, 1871

children were assigned their lot in life. Each child was given sufficient time and resources to accomplish the foreordained mission. The Lord reinforced that concept to Joseph Smith when He revealed: "For there is a time appointed for every man, according as his works shall be."[17]

Some spirit children had qualified for greater responsibilities here on earth by their diligence in the pre-earth life. Those noble spirit children foreordained to play a leading role during the last dispensation were formulated into the tribe of Ephraim even in the pre-earth life. Their assignment was to prepare the world for the Second Coming of Christ. They had the task of spreading the gospel to the rest of Father's children. They were given the responsibility in these last days to gather in the scattered remnants of the House of Israel. They had the responsibility of providing an opportunity for both the living and those who died without a knowledge of the saving ordinances of the gospel. They were indeed chosen. Chosen to wear out their lives offering salvation to the rest of the Children of Israel. Their promised rewards were both temporal and spiritual. They were to receive assistance from heavenly beings enabling them to accomplish their super-human task. However, whereas Ephraim would diligently throw himself into his assigned work, the Adversary, likewise, would do all in his power to thwart these children of the noble birthright. We will discuss Satan's opposition to Ephraim in the latter-days in Chapter 8. In the mantime we turn to a discussion of the Biblical Ephraim.

---

[17] D&C 121:25

CHAPTER 2

The Biblical Ephraim –
Son of Joseph

Joseph, the favored son of Israel who was sold into Egypt, rose to power in the Egyptian government and was given Asenath, the daughter of Potipher, priest of On, to be his wife (Gen. 41:45).[18] She bore two sons unto Joseph, the first was named Manasseh and the second Ephraim.

Biblical Names

The names of the children are significant. Bible scholars suggest that the parents believed the names given were received by revelation, foretelling what the child's role in this life would be. In other words, "In biblical thought a name is not a mere label of identification; it is an expression of the essential nature of its bearer. A man's name reveals his character."[19] For example, the name of Ishmael, son of Abraham and Hagar, was revealed to Hagar by an angel (Genesis 16:11-12); Isaac's name was revealed to Abraham by God (Genesis 17:19); and the Lord revealed to Rebekah the character of her twin sons (Genesis 25:22-26). The names Esau and Jacob given to the twin boys reflect another dimension of scholars' thinking regarding names. Names were "supposed to indicate some characteristics of the person; of the circumstances, trivial or momentous, connected with his or her birth, of the hopes, beliefs, or feelings of the parents."[20] The Genesis account implies that the names Esau and Jacob reflect the circumstances of their birth. Genesis also associates the

---

[18] Asenath was a descendant of Shem, her father was a priest in the Hyksos dynasty. See Answers to Gospel Questions 1:169-171.

[19] Buttrick, George A. et al The Interpreters Dictionary of the Bible, Abingdom Press, Nashville, 1962, p. 500.

[20] Hastings Dictionary of the Bible. Revised edition by Frederick C. Grant and H.H. Rowley, Charles Scribner's sons, New York, 1963, p. 687.

naming of all of Jacob's children with the feelings of the mother (see Genesis 29:32-30:24). Manasseh's name apparently reflected the feelings of Joseph "For God hath made me forget all my toil, and all my father's house" (Genesis 41:51). Joseph called the second son Ephraim, "For God hath caused me to be fruitful in the land of my affliction" (Genesis 41:52, see also 46:20). The name Ephraim was probably carefully selected and could be viewed as revelatory. Although today many would consider the name and the character or future of the child as coincidental, in Ephraim's case it proves to be a foretelling of not only Ephraim's, but his posterity's role in time to come. Jacob's and Moses' blessing concerning him will verify that his name was indeed revelatory.

Jacob Blesses Joseph's Sons

There is no further mention of Ephraim and Manasseh in the book of Genesis until Joseph was told that his father Jacob was sick and he (Joseph) took the two sons with him to visit his ailing father (Genesis 48:1). Upon being told of Joseph's approach, Jacob revived somewhat and spoke to his son Joseph of God's promise to him (Jacob) to become a multitude of people and to have the land of Canaan for an everlasting possession for his seed (Genesis 48:2-4). Adding to this background, Jacob informed Joseph that his two sons who had been born in Egypt were considered to be Jacob's sons even as were Reuben and Simeon, the two eldest sons of Jacob.

> And now, *of* thy two sons, Ephraim and Manasseh, which were born unto thee in the land of Egypt, before I came unto thee into Egypt; behold, they are mine, *and the God of my fathers shall bless them; even* as Reuben and Simeon they shall *be blessed, for they are mine; wherefore they shall be called after my name. (Therefore they were called Israel).*

> And thy issue which thou begettest after them, shall be thine, and shall be called after the name of their brethren in their inheritance, *in the tribes; therefore they were called the tribes of Manasseh and of Ephraim* (JST Genesis 48: 5-6).

The adoption of Joseph's two sons as "sons of Jacob" has led to much speculation as to where they fit into the twelve tribes of Israel. The various theories need not be reviewed here; suffice it to say that Joseph is no longer counted as a tribe, but his two sons, Ephraim and Manasseh, became numbered as tribes of Israel (see Numbers 2:18-20) making a total of thirteen. However, Levi's descendants were later spread among all the other twelve tribes and were not counted as a separate tribe thus reducing the number to twelve.

The Levites were called to officiate in the services of the tabernacle in place of the firstborn of all the families of Israel (Numbers 8:15-16, 19, 24-25). This stewardship was apparently given to the Levites because of their support of Moses when he came down from Mount Sinai and found the children of Israel worshiping the golden calf (Exodus 32:25-29). Although their assignment was given long after the adoption of Joseph's two sons by Jacob, when the number of the tribes of Israel became the same as the number of Jacob's sons, the revelatory nature of Jacob's blessing is further verified.

As Jacob continued his conversation with his son Joseph, he reminded him of God appearing to him and covenanting to give him and his seed the land (of Canaan) as an everlasting possession (JST Genesis 48:7). Jacob then recognized Joseph's contribution to the fulfilling of the covenant.

Therefore, O my son, he hath blessed me in raising thee up to be a servant unto me, in saving my house from death;

In delivering my people, thy brethren, from famine which was sore in the land; wherefore the God of thy fathers shall bless thee, and the fruit of thy loins, that they shall be blessed above thy brethren, and above thy father's house; (JST Genesis 48:8-9).

As the above blessing of Jacob to Joseph states, the promises extended to his posterity. Joseph had been shown in a dream when he was yet a lad that his brothers would bow down to him (Genesis 37: 5-10). Jacob now, under the inspiration of the Lord, proclaimed that the dream shown to Joseph would extend from generation to generation.

For thou hast prevailed, and thy father's house hath bowed down unto thee, even as it was shown unto thee, before thou wast sold into Egypt by the hands of thy brethren; wherefore thy brethren shall bow down unto thee, from generation to generation, unto the fruit of thy loins for ever;

For thou shalt be a light unto my people, to deliver them in the days of their captivity, from bondage; and to bring salvation unto them, when they are altogether bowed down under sin (JST Genesis 48:10-11).

A careful analysis of these verses shows that the blessings promised to Joseph's seed extended to all of his posterity through to the last days of the earth and into eternity.

The conversation between Joseph and Jacob had apparently taken place without Jacob noticing that Joseph's two sons had accompanied him there even though he had spoken specifically of them (Genesis 48:8-9). The oversight was probably because of his age. Jacob "could not see" (Genesis 48:10), in spite of the fact that Joseph had laid his hands upon him and healed his eyesight. This event, of course, had been shown to Jacob by God in the visions of the night before he went down to Egypt from the land of Canaan (Genesis 46:2-4). The healing of his eyesight had been seventeen years earlier (Genesis 47:28).

Having been told that the two lads were Joseph's sons, Jacob desired to bless them. Joseph guided the boys toward their grandfather with Manasseh the eldest being placed on Jacob's right side because he, naturally, was entitled to the birthright. However, Jacob knowingly placed his right hand on Ephraim and the left hand on Manasseh. Joseph endeavored to correct his father assuming he did not recognize who was the eldest (probably thinking the hands were placed mistakenly because of his poor eyesight), but Jacob assured him he knew what he was doing (Genesis 48:9-20). This is another evidence of Jacob's blessing being given by revelation.

The blessing given to the two young boys was an affirmation of what Jacob had previously told Joseph. The King James text says he blessed Joseph (v. 15), but as the footnote shows, the Septuagint (the Greek text copied from an earlier Hebrew text) states that he blessed "them." The blessing as recorded in the KJV was,

> God before whom my fathers Abraham and Isaac did walk, the God which fed me all my life long unto this day.

> The Angel which redeemed me from all evil, bless the lads; and let my name be named on them, and the name of my fathers Abraham and Isaac; and let them grow into a multitude in the midst of the earth (Genesis 48:15-16).

We call attention to two significant statements in the above blessing conferred upon the two sons of Joseph; 1) they were to have the name of Israel that had been given Jacob by the Angel who redeemed him[21]

---

[21] The angel who appeared was apparently Jehovah himself as a careful reading of the text and also Genesis 35:9-15 that speaks of a second appearance will confirm.

(Genesis 32:24-30), and; 2) the offspring of the two sons was to become a multitude of people in the midst of the earth. Joseph questioned his father regarding who was to inherit the birthright, having assumed Manasseh would. But Jacob responded; "I know it , my son, I know it: also he shall become a people, and also he shall be great: but truly his younger brother shall be greater then he, and his seed shall become a multitude of nations" (Genesis 48:19).

The King James text implies that the above words were not part of the blessing but an interpretation of what Jacob had said. Collectively the offspring of both sons would become a multitude. While Manasseh would become great, Ephraim would become even greater. Ephraim's greater blessing extended to his posterity who would become a multitude of nations. The "multitude of nations" may also be given a more enlightening translation. The word "nations" is often translated as "Gentiles."[22] The word multitude may also be translated "fulness."[23] Therefore, Ephraim's blessing as interpreted by Jacob could be that he would "become the fulness of the Gentiles." Nephi told us that when "the prophecies of Isaiah shall be fulfilled, man shall know of a surety, at the times when they come to pass," (2 Nephi 25:7). The same rule of interpretation would be applicable to scriptures other than Isaiah. When the Angel Moroni appeared to Joseph Smith in September, 1823, he "stated that the fulness of the Gentiles was soon to come in" (J.S. Hist. 1:41). The fulness of the Gentiles is the full opportunity for the nations of the Gentiles to receive the gospel (see D&C 45:24-30; JST Luke 21:24-32; 3 Nephi 16:7-11). The Prophet Joseph Smith, and other descendants of Ephraim, began the dispensation of taking the gospel to the Gentiles (D&C 21:10-12; 86:8-11; 90:6-9). Therefore, Ephraim is fulfilling the fulness of the Gentiles as stated by Moroni and as suggested in the translation of Genesis 48:19 above. Ephraim was scattered among all the nations of the Gentiles (Amos 9:8-9; Hosea 8:8).

Today Ephraim is being gathered out of those nations. As Ephraim is gathered, the Gentiles are being given an opportunity to accept the gospel and be numbered with Ephraim. When that gathering is completed, it will bring in the fulness of the Gentiles (See Chapter 3, Old Testament Prophets and Ephraim). We are living in the day of its fulfillment.

Jacob continued to bless the two sons following his brief interpretation to Joseph as noted above. He added: "In thee shall Israel (be) bless(ed),

---

[22] Dictionary of the Bible, Hastings, Revised Edition by Frederick C. Grant and H. H. Rowley, Charles Scribner & Sons N.Y., 1963, p. 689-90.

[23] See the dictionary synonyms for fulness: complete or attained all that is needed.

21

saying, God make thee as Ephraim and as Manasseh," (Genesis 48:20). Again the footnote and the Septuagint wording is significant, "Through thee (Ephraim and Manasseh) shall Israel be blessed." Their father Joseph had blessed the whole house of Israel as they had come and lived in Egypt. The blessing of Jacob to the two sons extended the role Joseph would play through his two sons, pertaining to futuristic blessings to the house of Israel.

Jacob's blessing of Ephraim before Manasseh was, in fact, designating him as the birthright holder. The birthright belongs to the eldest son unless otherwise revealed. Jacob had been given the birthright to replace his twin brother Esau (Genesis 27).[24] He understood the implications of the younger succeeding the elder. Jacob and Ephraim had been designated as the holder of the birthright by revelation (Genesis 25:23; 48:19-20). Ephraim was to succeed his father Joseph who had replaced Reuben as the holder of the birthright (1Chron. 5: 1-2; Jeremiah 31:9). Ephraim was the last birthright holder designated in the biblical text. As the servant of the Lord (birthright holder), he would bless the rest of the house of Israel in the latter days (D&C 133:32-34). This is the role of the birthright holder.

Following the blessing of Joseph's two sons, Jacob called all his sons together and blessed them regarding what would happen to them "in the last days" (Genesis 49:1). Although he blessed Joseph collectively, the blessings would have to be fulfilled through his only two sons Ephraim and Manasseh. Essentially Joseph was to have a fruitful posterity, and branches of the posterity would extend over the wall to the everlasting hills (the Americas). The blessing of Joseph was greater than his brothers (Genesis 49:22-26). The fulfillment of this blessing will be discussed in a later chapter.

There is no more said about Ephraim and Manasseh and their immediate posterity except that they lived in Egypt for three generations. "And Joseph dwelt in Egypt, he, and his father's house: and Joseph lived an hundred and ten years. And Joseph saw Ephraim's children of the third generation: the children also of Machir the son of Manasseh were brought up upon Joseph's knees" (Genesis 50:22-23). Unfortunately, there are no other reliable sources for this period of time.

Moses Blesses the Tribes of Israel

Joshua, a descendant of Ephraim, distinguished himself as one of the twelve spies sent to scout out the land of Canaan (Num. 13:1-25). He

---

[24] The details of Jacob obtaining the birthright will not be considered here. Undoubtedly the text is not complete. See D&C 132:37 for Jacob's worthiness to obtain the birthright and verification of his righteous living.

and Caleb, who was of the tribe of Judah, were the two spies who gave a true and favorable report of the land of Canaan. They were the only two of the entire older generation who came out of the land of Egypt, who were allowed to enter the promised land (Num. 14:6-39). After all of the tribes of Israel had wandered in the wilderness for forty years under Moses, they were allowed to go into the promised land of Canaan. However, Moses was not allowed to enter the land (Numbers 27:12-14; 20:7-13). Joshua was called and ordained to lead the children of Israel into the land (Num. 27:18-23).

The descendants of Ephraim and Manasseh as they came out of Egypt were considered as two of the tribes of Israel (Numbers 1:10[4-16]). Before Israel went over the Jordan into Canaan, Moses gave his last blessing to each of the tribes of Israel (Deut. 33). He blessed Joseph collectively but recognized them as two groups of people. The blessing is similar to the one Jacob gave Joseph as recorded in Genesis 49:22-26 as we have mentioned above.

And of Joseph he said, Blessed of the LORD be his land, for the precious things of heaven, for the dew, and for the deep that coucheth beneath,

And for the precious fruits brought forth by the sun, and for the precious things put forth by the moon,

And for the chief things of the ancient mountains, and for the precious things of the lasting hills,

And for the precious things of the earth and fulness thereof, and for the good will of him that dwelt in the bush: let the blessing come upon the head of Joseph, and upon the top of the head of him that was separated from his brethren (Deut. 33:13-16).

The above verses foretell again that Joseph's descendants were to migrate to the land of America. (Jesus gave the land of the Americas to the remnant of Joseph 3 Nephi 15:12-13). The unique blessing Moses gave to Ephraim and Manasseh follows: "His glory is like the firstling of his bullock, and his horns are like the horns of unicorns: with them he shall push the people together to the ends of the earth: and they are the ten thousands of Ephraim, and they are the thousands of Manasseh" (Deut. 33:17).

The comparison of Joseph's children to a bullock and a unicorn is significant. "The firstling of his bullock" is a designation of the birthright coming through Joseph to his children. A unicorn is a mythical one-horned animal. The Hebrew for unicorn, as noted in the footnote, is wild ox.[25]

The pushing of the people together to the ends of the earth is another way of foretelling the gathering of the house of Israel. The gathering from the ends of the earth signifies that the scattering was among all nations as Amos had prophesied (9:8-9). The ten thousands of Ephraim (the larger number further suggesting birthright) and the thousand of Manasseh could possibly designate those who will be gathered and/or those who will do the gathering. The words "with them" suggests that it will be Ephraim and Manasseh who will do the gathering. Of course many of Ephraim and Manasseh will be gathered first and then go out to gather from other nations. This interpretation is sustained in modern revelation where the Lord says the time will come (after Joseph's children are gathered) when the elders of the church "shall push the people together from the ends of the earth," (D&C 58:44-45).

We further note that one of the purposes of the revelations in the Doctrine and Covenants is to verify the fulfillment of the prophets (D&C 1:18). The elders of the Church are largely of Ephraim with a fewer number of Manasseh as Moses foretold. As they gather the people from the various nations, it will fulfill the previous blessing given to Ephraim by Jacob as interpreted above, Ephraim shall bring in "the fulness of the Gentiles" (Genesis 48:19).

This gathering is being fulfilled as we speak. Tens of thousands of Ephraim and thousands of Manasseh have been gathered and are today gathering many more including others of the tribes of Israel from the nations of the Gentiles.

Summary

The Bible does not give us much information on the mortal life of Ephraim or his brother Manasseh. It does record the role of their descendants. Ephraim as a tribe was foreordained to bless the rest of the house of Israel, particularly in the latter days. They were to gather the house of Israel who had been scattered among the Gentile nations and thus give the Gentiles an opportunity to accept the gospel and be numbered with Israel. This gathering will fulfill the covenant that God made to Abraham to bless all the kindreds of the earth (Genesis 12:1-3; Abraham 2:9-11). That blessing is being fulfilled today. The following chapters will give further evidence of this fulfillment.

---

[25] Joseph Smith changed the word unicorn in Isaiah 34:7 to wild ox in the JST. The change is an example of revelation to Joseph Smith being verified by modern scholarship.

CHAPTER 3

The Land Given to Ephraim

Nephi explained that one reason he understood Isaiah was because he had "dwelt at Jerusalem, wherefore (he knew) concerning the regions round about... (and) concerning the judgments of God which hath come to pass among the Jews" (2 Nephi 25:6). Similarly, we can better understand Ephraim by knowing the territory or the regions given to Ephraim. The "regions round about" refers to an understanding of the geography of the land of Canaan. "The judgments of God" has reference to what has happened to the people in that land as a result of their obeying or not obeying the commandments of God. Canaan was a land of promise. The same promise was undoubtedly extended to that land as was extended to the Americas: "Inasmuch as ye shall keep my commandments, ye shall prosper" (1 Nephi 2:20; see also Ether 2:9-10). A review of the geography and history of the people and territory of Ephraim will help us understand Ephraim in our own day. We will consider the territory of Ephraim in this chapter and in Chapter Four will analyze the history of Ephraim until they were scattered among the Gentiles.

The Geography

The children of Joseph are designated in the Book of Numbers as the children of Ephraim and the children of Manasseh. Thus, as stated in the previous chapter, Ephraim is numbered as one of the twelve tribes in place of Joseph. Manasseh is also numbered as a separate tribe (Num. 1:32-35), and is counted in place of Levi as we also noted previously. Ephraim and Manasseh were both assigned a territory in the land of Canaan by Joshua.[26] Ephraim was assigned the territory north of the

---

[26] Manasseh was given property on both sides of the Jordan, and his territory was the largest geographically of all the tribes. The territory given him on the west of the Jordan was bordered on the south by Ephraim (Numbers 32 and Joshua 16).

tribe of Benjamin, which was north of Jerusalem. The border on the east was the Jordan River and on the west was the country of the Philistines on the Mediterranean coast.[27] The major cities in the territory were Bethel, Shechem, and Shiloh. Bethel was on the southern border of Ephraim and although technically in the territory of Benjamin (Joshua 18:13,20), had an effect on the children of Ephraim. Shechem was near the northern border next to the territory of Manasseh (See I Chron. 7:28). Shiloh was between Shechem and Bethel. Major events in Old Testament times took place in all three of these cities.

The Divided Kingdom

The kingdom of Israel was divided into two nations after the death of King Solomon. Rehoboam was the king of the southern kingdom constituting the tribe of Judah and half of the tribe of Benjamin. Jeroboam was established as the king of the northern ten tribes.[28] The children of Ephraim became the leading tribe of the northern kingdom and, in fact, the kingdom was commonly known as the nation or kingdom of Ephraim among the prophetic and historical books of the Bible (for example see 2 Chron. 25:7; Isaiah 9: 9; 11:13). The territory also became known as Mount Ephraim (see various designations throughout Joshua and Judges) or the hill country of Ephraim in some translations because of the hilly country toward the east. In addition, there was a city called Ephraim within the territory of Ephraim, noteworthy for Jesus having visited the city prior to the last passover during his mortal ministry (John 11:54).

Bethel was near the southern border of the northern ten tribes where King Jeroboam set up one of the golden calves for the children of Israel to worship rather than going to Jerusalem for that purpose. The other calf was set up at the northern border city of Dan (1 Kings 12:28-29). Much earlier both Abraham and Jacob had built altars to worship at Bethel (Abr. 2:20; Genesis 28:10-22). Jacob had seen a vision of the three degrees of glory,[29] (each "round" of Jacob's ladder was symbolic of a degree of glory). Bethel, which means house of God, was named by Jacob and he vowed to build a house of God where he placed a stone for a pillar (Genesis 28:18-22). It is ironic that Jeroboam chose this sight as a place of false worship. However, it exemplifies what Joseph Smith

---

[27] See map 5 in the LDS Church edition of the KJV of the Bible.

[28] Technically, there were only 9 1/2 tribes. Simeon was absorbed into Judah (Joshua 19:1) and did not maintain a separate identity. Thus, the other nine tribes and the other half of Benjamin became known as the ten northern tribes.

[29] Teachings of the Prophet Joseph Smith, page 305.

taught: "In relation to the kingdom of God, the devil always sets up his kingdom at the very same time in opposition to God"[30] Although it was not set up at the same time, it was probably the devil influencing Jeroboam to set up the golden calf as an effort to desecrate the sacred city of Bethel.

Shiloh was the place where the sacred tabernacle, the portable temple, was established after the children of Israel had carried it through the wilderness for forty years. It was the place where the people went yearly to offer sacrifices (1 Sam. 1:3). It was the center of worship for the northern kingdom of Israel before the days of Jeroboam, and was, therefore, a type of the New Jerusalem to be set up as the center place of Zion in the latter-days (D&C 57:2-3).

Shechem was on the northern border of Ephraim and Manasseh. It was one of six cities given as a place of refuge for anyone guilty of or accused of manslaughter—they were to be given a fair trial under the law of Moses (Joshua 20). The Bible says the suburbs of Shechen were in mount Ephraim (Joshua 21:21). In other words it was located at the base of mount Gerizim and Mount Ebal, the two highest mountains of Mount Ephraim, where the children of Israel shouted the blessings and cursings attached to keeping or not keeping the laws of God as they dwelt in the land of Canaan (Deut. 27:11-26). Joshua was buried in Mount Ephraim after he had established the children of Israel in the land of Canaan, a fitting place for this courageous, faithful son of Ephraim (Joshua 24:29-30). The children of Israel brought the bones of Joseph out of Egypt and buried them in Shechem as they had promised to do (Genesis 50:24-25; Joshua 24:32).

Probably the most famous biblical event at Shechem (Sychar) was Jesus' conversation with the women of Samaria at Jacob's well, which had been dug almost two thousand years earlier. The woman's question was about worshiping God in the mountain (Gerazim). The Samaritans, a nation established through the intermarriage or grafting of Gentiles and Israelites (2 Kings 17:24), had established the mountain as a place of worship rather than going to Jerusalem because of the animosity between the Samaritans and the Jews. The Jews claimed the Samaritans had polluted their heritage by marrying Gentiles, but the Samaritans claimed their lineage also to be of the seed of Abraham. Jesus answered the question of where to worship by saying they must worship in spirit and in truth. The Jews had the truth but did not worship in the spirit. The Samaritans had the proper attitude or spirit of worship but did not

---

[30] Teachings of the Prophet Joseph Smith, page 365.

have the truth. Unknown to them, the coming judgments of God would prevent them from worshiping in either place (John 4:20-24). Jesus told his disciples that the Samaritan field was ripe, ready for harvest (John 4:34-38). The Gentile graft into the house of Israel (Jacob 5) had taken hold and produced good fruit. The disciples were to harvest the fruit when the appropriate time came.

There were many other cities and many biblical incidents connected with Ephraim, but the few examples above are evidence of the rich territorial heritage of the seed of Ephraim. Today, travel is limited in the territory because of the Arab-Israeli conflict; however, we have traveled through the territory several times in the last twenty-five years, and always have a special spiritual feeling as to the importance of the land given to Ephraim's ancestors.

CHAPTER 4

Ephraim and the Judgments of God

Many of the prophets foretold of the destruction and eventual gathering of the nation of Israel and of the scattering of the people of Ephraim. Hosea and Isaiah were two prophets who lived about the time of the conquest of Northern Israel by the Assyrians in 722 BC and warned Israel of the coming destruction and captivity of the people. Hosea warned Ephraim about their impending destruction over a fifty year period (about 777-726 BC), and Isaiah spent almost twenty years prophesying and warning Ephraim just prior to the Assyrian invasion (740-721 BC). Hosea gave the most extensive prophecies of any of the prophets regarding the northern kingdom which he labeled as Ephraim. Although many other prophets foretold of the scattering (and gathering) of Ephraim, our focus will be on those prophecies that specifically designate Ephraim as the northern nation of Israel.

Hosea is best known for the strange marriages that are recorded in the first three chapters of his book. The marriages are symbolic of the Lord's marriage or covenant with the house of Israel through which the children of Israel were to be born. Hosea is commanded to marry Gomer, a wife of whoredoms. The children born to this union, also recorded in the first three chapters, symbolically represent the scattering and gathering of Israel.[31]

The first prophecy of Hosea was represented in the first child of this marriage, a son named Jezreel (Hosea 1:4), the downfall of Northern Israel was to take place in this famous valley which was then ripening in iniquity.

The second child born to Hosea and Gomer was a daughter (Hosea 1:6-7). God commanded that she be named Lo-ruhamah. The name means, as the text states, that God will no longer extend mercy to the

---

[31] The symbolism of the marriage will not be discussed here. For further analysis, see Sydney B. Sperry, The Voice of Israel's Prophet, Deseret Book Co. 1952, p. 290, or Farres H. Nyman, The Words of the Twelve Prophets, Deseret Book Co. 1991, p. 22-25.

nation of Israel but will take it away. The first prophecy had foretold the downfall of Ephraim as a nation and the second prophecy adds the dimension that some of the tribe members would be taken into captivity.

The third child of the prophet and his wife was a boy. The child's name was to be Lo-ammi, which signifies that Israel is no longer recognized as the Lord's people (Hosea 1:8-9). He will no longer be their God. Jehovah had promised Moses in Egypt that Israel would be his people and he would be their God (Exodus 6:7). He was now rescinding that covenant because Israel had not lived up to its conditional agreements (Deut. 4:25-28).

Chapter Three is considered by many as a second marriage into which Hosea is commanded to enter. In our opinion, it is not a second marriage but a specific lesson given to Hosea concerning the first marriage—it is a symbolic representation or application of the first marriage. Hosea's command to love an adulteress who looks to other gods is an admonition. Hosea is to love Israel and teach the people as long as anyone will listen to him (Hosea 3:1). The purchase of the woman for the fifteen pieces of silver plus barley is symbolic of the Lord's taking his people out of their adulterous situation of worshiping another god and placing them in another environment. They would not only be taken out of the Lord's presence, but away from Baal, the pagan god, where they could no longer play the harlot through false worship (Hosea 3:2). The value of the silver and barley has been explained in various ways but none of the explanations have been confirmed by revelation, to our knowledge. There is undoubtedly some significance attached to the total price which someday will be understood. It probably symbolic of Christ's atonement to pay for the sins of Israel.

Since Israel has been purchased by the Lord, it is now his prerogative to do with her as he sees appropriate. Her punishment is set. She is to be taken away where she cannot worship Baal (Hosea 3:3). This was fulfilled by her being taken into captivity by Assyria and then scattered or taken further into the north. From the Apocryphal writings (which the Lord said "there are many things contained therein that are true, and it is mostly translated correctly" (D&C 91:1), we read about the pending doom of the people of Ephraim or the people of the Northern Kingdom.

These are the ten tribes which were led away from their own land into captivity in the days of King Hoshea, whom Shalmaneser the king of the Assyrians led captive; he took them across the river, and they were taken into another land. But they formed this plan for themselves, that they would leave the multitude of the nations and go to a more distant region, where mankind had never lived, that there at least they might keep their statutes which they had not kept in their own land.

And they went in by the narrow passages of the Euphrates river.

For at the time the Most High performed signs for them, and stopped the channels of the river until they had passed over. Through that region there was a long way to go, a journey of a year and a half; and that country is called Arzareth.

Then they dwelt there until the last times; and now, when they are about to come again, the Most High will stop the channels of the river again, so that they may be able to pass over. Therefore you saw the multitude gathered together in peace.

But those who are left of your people, who are found within my holy borders, shall be saved. (2 Esdras 13:40-48).[32]

The length of time between their being taken captive into Assyria and going into the north is not given in 2 Esdras. However, Isaiah foretold the exact time of Ephraim going into the north, "within three score and five (65) years" of the time he warned king Ahaz of Judah not to worry about the threatened invasion of Syria and Ephraim upon Judah (about 734 B.C.). Apparently the ten tribes remained in Assyria for some time, and then went further into the north. The locality of the ten tribes was not known after they went into the north thus fulfilling Isaiah's prophecy, "shall Ephraim be broken, that it be not a people" (Isaiah 7:8). As they went north the prophecy of Amos was also fulfilled.

The Lord declared that his eyes were upon the sinful kingdom of Northern Israel and it will be destroyed from off the face of the earth. Although the nation will be removed, the people will not all be eliminated. As previously prophesied (JST Amos 7:3,6), the house of Jacob was not to be utterly destroyed. They were, however, to be sifted among all nations, as corn (wheat) is sifted in a sieve, but every kernel of that corn will be accounted for by the Lord who knows all things.

---

[32] For an explanation of the book called the Apocrypha see the Bible Dictionary in the LDS edition of the Bible, p. 610. It is recommended that the entire 91st section of the Doctrine and Covenants be read also.

Behold, the eyes of the Lord GOD are upon the sinful kingdom, and I will destroy it from off the face of the earth; saving that I will not utterly destroy the house of Jacob, saith the Lord.

For, lo, I will command, and I will sift the house of Israel among all nations, like as corn is sifted in sieve, yet shall not the least grain fall upon the earth (Amos 9:8-9).

President Spencer W. Kimball, in a First Presidency Message, quoted this passage with a slightly modified ending that verified our interpretation here. Said he: "Yet the Lord has not forgotten Israel, for though Israel was to be sifted among all nations, the Lord nevertheless said, 'Yet shall not the least grain fall upon the earth' *and be lost*" (Amos 9:9, italics added).[33] Just as one sparrow shall not fall to the ground without the knowledge of God (Matthew 10:29-31), the house of Israel, who were numbered in the days of the separation of the sons of Adam (Deuteronomy 32:8), are of more value to the Father than a sparrow.

His program of scattering Israel among all the nations of the earth was for two purposes: to benefit of Israel, and to benefit all the nations among whom they were to be scattered. In their state of wickedness, Israel needed to be separated from each other and purged of her iniquities through living among other peoples. While the other people did not have the gospel in its fulness, they did have customs and moral values to help make Israel a more honorable people. As subsequent generations came along, there were prophetic promises made that the time would come when the gospel would be preached again upon the earth, and those of the house of Israel (the wheat) who were living among the Gentiles (the tares) would accept the gospel and become a part of fulfilling the covenant made to Abraham, Isaac, and Jacob.[34]

Those who were valiant in their premortal life would recognize the message of the gospel. As Jesus said in the gospels, "My sheep hear my voice, and I know them, and they follow me" (John 10:27, compare D&C 29:7).

As the restoration unfolds, those to whom the keys and authority would be given are commissioned to teach the gospel to the world. As they go among the various nations of the earth, those of the blood of

---

[33] Kimball, Spencer W. Ensign, Dec. 1975, pg. 4.

[34] See D&C 86 for the justification of equating the house of Israel with the wheat and the Gentiles with the tares. After clarifying the parable of the wheat and the tares (Matt. 13:24-30), the Lord tells the priesthood holders of the newly restored church that they "are lawful heirs, according to the flesh" (literal seed of Abraham, Isaac, and Jacob [your fathers v.8]), the house of Israel or wheat that "have been hid from the world (among the tares) with Christ in God" (v.9).

Israel are gathered together. Those who are not of the blood of Israel are given the opportunity to come in and be adopted or numbered with Israel (3 Nephi 30:1-2). Through this procedure, the covenant made to Abraham is fulfilled that through him would " all families of the earth be blessed" (Genesis 12:3; Abraham 2:9-10).

In their scattered condition, Israel would abide many days without a king, a prince, a sacrifice, an image, an ephod or a teraphim (Hosea 3:4). This is another way of saying they will have no priesthood or political leadership from Christ, no ordinances or spiritual leadership of the church, and no revelation. The ephod and teraphim were instruments associated with revelation. In other words, the people would be in a state of apostasy for many days.

The fourth chapter of Hosea enumerates several causes of the scattering of Ephraim. Our purpose is not to analyze these causes but to show that she was scattered. The chapter does identify Ephraim as a nation and in the same verse summarizes a major cause for her scattering and the condition that will follow. "Ephraim is joined to idols: let (her) alone" (Hosea 4:17).

In Hosea Chapter Five, the Lord continues to chasten Ephraim. That Hosea is addressing Ephraim as a nation is evidenced by the many references to her. Seven of the first fourteen verses in Chapter Five refer to Ephraim. Some of these references are used in negative similitudes, a pattern followed in future chapters that is often very picturesque. The Lord says, "I know Ephraim, and Israel is not hid from me (the Lord knows her wickedness): for now, O Ephraim, thou committest whoredom, and Israel is defiled" (5:3). He gives another cause of her fall. "And the pride of Israel doth testify to his face: therefore shall Israel and Ephraim fall in their iniquity" (5:5). Had Ephraim taken heed to the scriptural Proverb: "Pride goeth before destruction, and an haughty spirit before a fall" (Proverb 16:18), they could have avoided their captivity. Isaiah calls them the drunkards of Ephraim and prophecies that "the crown of pride, the drunkards of Ephraim, shall be trodden down" (Isaiah 28:1-4).

Again making known his omniscience, the Lord, through Hosea, declared: "Ephraim shall be desolate in the day of rebuke: among the tribes of Israel have I made known that which shall surely be" (Hosea 5:9). She had not sinned ignorantly, "Ephraim is oppressed and broken in judgment, because (she) willingly walked after the commandment," or after filth as stated in the footnote (Hosea 5:11).

Using negative similies, the Lord says he will "be unto Ephraim as a moth" (Hosea 5:12). Moths destroy clothes as the Lord will destroy Ephraim. Ephraim had recognized her sickness and went to Assyria for help instead of the Lord. Because of her wickedness the Lord "will be unto Ephraim as a lion," he "will tear and go away; (he) will take away, and none shall rescue" Ephraim (Hosea 5:13-14). The fall of Judah mentioned in the verses that follow along here and hereafter will not be considered because we are dealing with Ephraim. The message is primarily a description of Ephraim's wickedness and predicted fall.

Hosea's fifth chapter concludes with the Lord declaring that he will return to his place until Ephraim acknowledges her sins and seeks him (Hosea 5:15). Apparently Ephraim's descendants did not seek the Lord through the long years of the apostasy, for the Lord does not dwell in unholy temples of individuals or nations (Alma 7:21).

Chapters seven through ten give many more negative similies in describing the downfall of Ephraim. The fall of Judah is also periodically mentioned. A verse-by-verse analysis is not necessary here to understand the main concept of Ephraim being mixed among the Gentiles after she is taken captive (Hosea 8:8), but a few of the similitudes will be considered.

In the negative similitudes, Ephraim's scattering is compared to a cake not turned because she had mixed herself among the people (Hosea 7:8). In other words, Ephraim had embraced the culture of the strangers (Canaanites). The Canaanites had not been driven out of the land as the Lord had commanded (Judges 1:29). Ephraim had become "of the world" instead of "in the world but not of it." She was cooked on only one side to the degree that her strength had been sapped and she did not turn to the Lord (Hosea 7:9-10). A pancake cooked on only one side is not edible: Ephraim's wickedness left her undesirable to the Lord, so she was scattered.

Ephraim is also compared to a silly dove without a heart: they call to Egypt, they go to Assyria (Hosea 7:11). A dove is to return or call to her master, but Ephraim looks elsewhere rather than to the Lord. However, the Lord will deal with her through the Assyrian conquest. Following other comparisons and descriptions of their wickedness (Hosea chapters 8-10), they are prophesied to be "swallowed up, now shall they be among the Gentiles as a vessel wherein is no pleasure," "God will cast them away, because they did not hearken unto him: and they shall be wanderers among the nations" (Hosea 8:8; 9:17). Thus, today as people are gathered into The Church of Jesus Christ of Latter-day Saints or as the remnants of Israel are gathered from among the nations of the Gentiles and other nations, it should be no surprise to find patriarchal blessings declaring these people to be of the blood of Ephraim.

Some scholars have interpreted Hosea 12:3-4, in which the birth of Jacob, the father of the house of Israel, and his subsequent wrestle with an angel (Genesis 32:24-29) are described, to be a declaration of Jacob's deceptive nature or the beginning of Israel's waywardness. We believe, however, that there is another interpretation of this passage. It shows that Jacob was strong from the beginning and prevailed in his mortal probation. However, Jacob's strength will not save his posterity. Each person and each nation will be judged individually (Hosea 12:2) in light of warnings given through his prophets (2 Ne. 25:9; 2 Kings 17:13).

Ephraim as a nation departed from the Lord, in spite of the Lord's guidance through visions and prophets and his taking Jacob out of the wicked land of Canaan and sending him to Syria to obtain a wife of the covenant (Hosea 12:7-12). The Lord also raised up a prophet (Moses) to lead Israel out of Egypt, but Ephraim had by then provoked the Lord to anger (Hosea 12:13-14).

Hosea Chapter Thirteen declares Ephraim's demise. Ephraim prospered when she followed the Lord but died when she followed Baal. Ephraim is now sinning more and more (Hosea 13:1-2). Because of Ephraim's sins, she has destroyed herself and none can help her but the Lord (Hosea 13:9-14).

In addition to Hosea, Isaiah, and Amos as quoted above, traditional dating would list Joel, Jonah, and Micah as having prophesied during this time also.

Finally, Isaiah had been called to warn Ephraim, "Until the cities be wasted without inhabitant, and the house without man, and the land be utterly desolate, and the Lord have removed men far away, and there be a great forsaking in the midst of the land" (Isaiah 6:11-12). Isaiah's mission was now complete, the Assyrians destroyed the nation, literally shaved the land (Isaiah 7:20), and took the more righteous or the less wicked out of the land into the north. As the Lord told Jeremiah, "I have cast out all your brethren (of Judah), even the whole seed of Ephraim" (Jeremiah 7:15). Ephraim was destined to wait until the times of the gathering of Ephraim in the latter days.

CHAPTER 5

Biblical Prophecies Concerning the Gathering of Ephraim

Nephi said that Isaiah was "hard for many of (his) people to understand; for they know not concerning the manner of prophesying among the Jews" (2 Nephi 25:1). One of Isaiah's seemingly obvious ways of prophesying was to give a message of doom but always follow it with a message of hope. The messages of hope pertained to Israel's future gathering, that is the gathering in our day and time. Most of the Old Testament prophets followed the same manner of prophesying. The interpretation of the Old Testament prophecies discussed in this chapter will be further verified by modern-day prophets interpretations included in later chapters of this work and will not be included here.

Hosea, Prophet of Ephraim

The first prophecies of Hosea are prophecies of doom upon Ephraim or Israel pronounced through the birth of the first three children born unto Gomer, Hosea's wife of harlotry. As discussed in Chapter Four, these births were symbolic of the destruction and scattering of Israel. However, to understand the message of hope that follows, we must remember that God's covenant with Abraham was that his offspring would be as numberless as the sand of the sea (Genesis 22:17). The Lord affirms, through Hosea, that this promise of Abraham is still in effect and will yet be fulfilled, in spite of the destruction and captivity of Ephraim.

Yet the number of the children of Israel shall be as the sand of the sea, which cannot be measured nor numbered; and it shall come to pass, that in the place where it was said unto them, ye are not my people, there it shall be said unto them, Ye are the sons of the living God.

Then shall the children of Judah and the children of Israel be gathered together, and appoint themselves one head, and they shall come up out of the land: for great shall be the day of Jezreel (Hosea 1:10-11).

The people of Israel were told that they were not "God's people," but they will again be gathered and told they are the sons of the living God. This promise constitutes a restoration of the gospel and the authority to perform ordinances. Becoming the son or daughter of the living God comes through the ordinance of water baptism and the baptism of fire and the Holy Ghost, or spiritual adoption (Mosiah 5:7). These ordinances were to be extended to Israel in the last days. The prophecy expands to include Judah. When Israel is gathered again, Judah will be likewise, and the kingdoms will be no longer divided. They will be under one head of government, the kingdom of God (Hosea 1:11). Paul recognized this as a prophecy to the Gentiles (Romans 9:24-26). Since Israel was to be scattered among the Gentiles, they would eventually be gathered out. The gathering out of the [other] land(s) will be a great day for Jezreel, or the nation of Israel.

Isaiah also foretold of a second gathering of Israel. The Angel Moroni quoted the Eleventh Chapter of Isaiah to Joseph Smith and said it "was about to be fulfilled" (J.S.-Hist. 1:40). Part of Isaiah's prophecy stated: "And it shall come to pass in that day, that the Lord shall set his hand again the second time to recover the remnant of his people, which shall be left, from Assyria, and from Egypt, and from Pathros, and from Cush, and from Elam, and from Shinar, and from Hamath, and from the islands of the sea" (Isaiah 11:11).

The Lord's setting his hand the second time to recover his people pertains to the bringing forth of The Book of Mormon. Nephi said,

But behold, there shall be many- at that day when I shall proceed to do a marvelous work among them, that I may remember my covenants which I have made unto the children of men, that I may set my hand again the second time to recover my people, which are of the house of Israel;

And also, that I may remember the promises which I have made unto thee, Nephi, and also unto thy father, that I would remember your seed; and that the words of your seed should proceed forth out of my mouth unto your seed; and my words shall hiss forth unto the ends of the earth, for a standard unto my people, which are of the house of Israel. (2 Nephi 29:1-2)

The Book of Mormon is the instrument of the Lord to bring about the gathering of Israel.

The prophet Joseph Smith interpreted the recovering of the remnants of Abraham, Isaac, and Jacob from among the nations (Isaiah 11:11) as the bringing in of the fulness of the Gentiles and offering the covenant of Abraham to them (the Gentiles) as well[35]. The remnants who are recovered would, of course, be the seed of those (House of Israel) who had been scattered among the Gentiles.

Jeremiah also foretold the second gathering of Israel. Comparing the second gathering to Moses bringing the children of Israel out of Egypt, he prophesied,

> Therefore, behold, the days come, saith the LORD, that it shall no more be said, The LORD liveth, that brought up the children of Israel out of the land of Egypt:
>
> But, The LORD liveth, that brought up the children of Israel from the land of the north, and from all the lands whither he had driven them: and I will bring them again into their land that I gave unto their fathers. (Jeremiah 16:14-15)

The scattering (Exodus) of more than two million people of the house of Israel from bondage was an event spoken of for thousands of years, and it is still referred to by believing Jews and Christians as one of the Lord's greatest miracles for his people. However, the gathering of millions of the tribes of Israel is also one of the Lord's greatest miracles. There are yet millions more who will be gathered.

Jeremiah also foretold how the gathering would be done.

> Behold, I will send for many fishers, saith the LORD, and they shall fish them; and after will I send for many hunters, and they shall hunt them from every mountain, and from every hill, and out of the holes of the rocks.
>
> For mine eyes are upon all their ways: they are not hid from my face, neither is their iniquity hid from mine eyes (Jeremiah 16:16-17).

First the Lord will send for many fishers; then he will send for many hunters. Fishing in the days of Jeremiah was done with nets and schools

---

[35] Smith, Joseph Fielding, <u>Teaching of the Prophet Joseph Smith</u>, p. 14.

of fish were caught. In the early days of the Church, the missionaries went to the various locations and preached to congregations, or invited all interested people to assemble in the local schoolhouses, or community halls. Ofttimes, whole groups of people were converted. The conversion of these groups would fulfill Jeremiah's prophecy of fishing.

The hunting period would follow the fishing period of missionary work as foretold by Jeremiah. Hunting is done on a one-on-one basis. Later the Church missionary program changed from the teaching of groups to the teaching of individuals or families as is presently done and further fulfills Jeremiah's prophecy. Oliver Cowdery reported that the Angel Moroni quoted Jeremiah 16:16 as one which was soon to be fulfilled.[36] Verse seventeen is the Lord's declaration that he knows where the house of Israel has been scattered (the same concept as expressed in Amos 9:9 quoted above). Verses 19-20 foretells the Gentiles being given an opportunity to come in and be numbered with Israel, and partake of the blessings of the children of Israel.

Hosea Chapter Two describes the gathering of Ephraim from their scattered condition among the Gentiles. "Say ye unto your brethren, Ammi; and to your sisters, Ruhamah" (Hosea 2:1). The children are now designated as Ammi and Ruhamah. The Lo, which means no in Hebrew, is dropped. The Lord is saying that the children of Israel are once again to be his people and obtain mercy. Those who are called his people and have obtained mercy are to plead with their mother. "Plead with your mother, plead: for she is not my wife, neither am I her husband: let her therefore put away her whoredoms out of her sight, and her adulteries from between her breasts" (Hosea 2:2). The plea to the mother seems to refer to those of Israel who are gathered and then have the responsibility to gather the rest of the house of Israel. It is the same message as Isaiah 52:11, the calling of Israel out from among the Gentiles. "Depart ye, depart ye, go ye out from thence, touch no unclean thing; go ye out of the midst of her; be ye clean, that bear the vessels of the Lord" (Isaiah 52:11).

Hosea's prophecy also carries the same message as another prophecy of Isaiah.

> And said unto me, Thou art my servant, O Israel, in whom I will be glorified... And he said, It is a light thing that thou shouldest be my servant to raise up the tribes of Jacob, and to restore the preserved of Israel: I will also give thee for a light to the Gentiles, that thou mayest be my salvation unto the end of the earth. (Isaiah 49:3, 6)

---

[36] Messenger and Advocate, April 1835, p. 111.

The people of Israel, as the gathered servants, are to raise up the tribes of Jacob and restore the preserved of Israel (among the Gentiles). As they gather the preserved of Israel, they will also give the Gentiles an opportunity to be numbered with Israel and further fulfill the Lord's covenant with Abraham that his seed would bless the nations of the Gentiles (Genesis 12:3; 1 Nephi 22:9). Thus, in the context of Hosea, Ammi and Ruhamah represent the small gathered remnant children who are to plead with the mother of Israel representing the vast number of the body of Israel.

Mother Israel is invited by the Lord to forsake her unfaithful and sinful practices—the worshiping of other gods, or symbolically having an affair with someone other than her husband, Jehovah (Hosea 2:2-5). Because Israel has followed other gods, she will not prosper and shall fail to find satisfaction in spiritual endeavors of these other gods. This will cause her to turn to her first husband, Jehovah, but she will have a period in which she will not prosper (Hosea 1:6-13). Following this unprosperous period, the Lord will bring Israel into the wilderness and speak to her or gather her and give her revelation.

At that day, Israel will recognize the Lord as her husband or her God (Ishi; see footnote to Hosea 2:16) and not call upon the names of Baalim (Hosea 2:14-17). The Lord will bless Israel and reinstate his marriage and she shall know the Lord. God will again have mercy on Israel and be her God and Israel will recognize him as her God. The gathering of Israel following the scattering is thus foretold through Hosea. This interpretation is strengthened through Paul's quoting Hosea 2:23 as a promise to be fulfilled to the Gentiles (Romans 9:25). Jeremiah gave a similar prophecy to Hosea. He spoke of the Gentiles worshiping false gods.

> O LORD, my strength, and my fortress, and my refuge in the day of affliction, the Gentiles shall come unto thee from the ends of the earth, and shall say, Surely our fathers have inherited lies, vanity, and things wherein there is no profit.
>
> Shall a man make gods unto himself, and they are no gods?
>
> Therefore, behold, I will this once cause them to know, I will cause them to know mine hand and my might; and they shall know that my name is The Lord. (Jeremiah 16:19-21)

Oliver Cowdery reported that the Angel Moroni also included this prophecy of Jeremiah among those soon to be fulfilled.

41

And it will come to pass, that though the house of Israel has forsaken the Lord, and bowed down and worshiping other gods, which were no gods, and been cast out before the face of the world, they will know the voice of the Shepherd when he calls upon them this time; for soon his day of power comes, and in it his people will be willing to harken to his counsel; and even now are they already beginning to be stirred up in their hearts to search for these things, and are daily reading the ancient prophets, and are marking the times, and seasons of their fulfillment, Thus God is preparing the way for their return.

But it is necessary that you should understand, that what is to be fulfilled in the last days, Is not only for the benefit of Israel, but the Gentiles, if they will repent and embrace the gospel, for they are to be remembered also in the same covenant, and are to be fellow heirs with the seed of Abraham, inasmuch as they are so by faith—for God is no respecter of persons.[37]

The Lord has still more to say through Hosea concerning his marriage to Israel. It is another message of hope. After some time, Israel shall return and seek the Lord, and David their king. "Afterward shall the children of Israel return, and seek the LORD their God, and David their king; and shall fear the LORD and his goodness in the latter days" (Hosea 3:5). This will be fulfilled in the latter days (Hosea 3:5). "The Lord their God" and "David their king" has reference to the same person, Jesus the Christ. There will be a spiritual and a political restoration to Israel bringing about the full kingdom of God. The reference to Jesus as David is one of many among the Old Testament prophets.[38] Thus, Hosea Chapter Three describes, as does Chapter Two, Ephraim's captivity, dispersion, and subsequent restoration.

The causes of Ephraim's downfall were given in Hosea Chapters Four and Five. The Sixth Chapter begins with Israel saying, "Come, and let us return unto the Lord" (Hosea 6:1). The rest of the verse implies that Israel's statement is made after a lengthy period of her being smitten or punished. The following verse gives a time frame for their return. "After

---

[37] Messenger and Advocate, April 1835, p. 111. It is not clear whether Oliver is quoting the Angel Moroni, paraphrasing him, giving his own commentary, or giving a combination of quoting and paraphrasing. Nevertheless, the concepts come from the angel.

[38] This work will not treat the full kingdom of God. Suffice it to say that Christ is the David spoken of who will reign politically during the millennium. For a fuller account, see Millennial Messiah, McConkie, Bruce R., p. 591-601. Other prophets' references to David include: Jeremiah 23:5-6; Ezekial 34:23; 37:22-28. See also D&C 58:22.

two days will he revive us: in the third day he will raise us up, and we shall live in his sight" (Hosea 6:2).

While some look upon this verse as a prophecy of Christ's resurrection, and of course all things have their likeness and bear record of him (Moses 6:63), the context suggests the verse is speaking of the nation of Israel. The <u>New International Version of the Bible</u> (hereafter NIV) supports the interpretation of his speaking of Israel: "After two days he will revive us; *on* the third day he will *restore* us, that we may live in his *presence*" (Italics added). A day with the Lord is a thousand years with man (Psalms 90:4; 2 Peter 3:8; Abraham 5:13; facs. #2, fig. 1). Therefore, in the Lord's time, two days equals 2000 years. In the third day could be any part of the next thousand years. Israel was taken away in 721 B.C. It was about 2550 years from the time of Israel's destruction and scattering until the restoration in 1830, a period of two days and the third day of the Lord's time.

Furthermore, two thousand years from 721 B. C. would be about the end of the Thirteenth Century A.D. (1279). This date is approximately the ending of the dark ages and the beginning of the age of Enlightenment. The Enlightenment is possibly the Lord beginning to revive Israel but would not raise her up for part of another day, after the Renaissance and the Reformation. They shall again live in his sight (Hosea 6:2).[39] Other Old Testament prophets have foretold of these sequential events (Isaiah 28:23-29).

The next verse describes the time when Israel comes to know the Lord (Hosea 6:3). This verse also fits the period following the restoration of the Church and encompasses the Church's growth in the knowledge of the Lord.

In the rest of Chapter Six, the Lord laments over Israel and Judah's transgressions of the covenant they had made with him. In this lamentation, one of the more well-known verses in Hosea is recorded. "For I desired mercy, and not sacrifice; and the knowledge of God more than burnt offerings" (Hosea 6:6). The Savior quotes it twice during his ministry to refute the self-righteous Pharisees (Matt. 9:13; 12:7). The Lord is more interested in how people relate to each other and come to a

---

[39] In 1843, the Prophet Joseph Smith used Hosea 6:2 as an evidence that the second coming of Christ would not be before the year 1890: "After two days, etc., – 2,520 years" (<u>TPJS</u>, p. 286). Unfortunately, his discussion that explained the total years as 2520 years was summarized merely as an "etc."

Subtracting 2520 years from 1890 brings one to the year 630 B.C. While this year does not seem to figure into Hosea's lifetime, it is evidence that Joseph considered the prophecy to be fulfilled in the latter days and not as a prophecy of Christ's resurrection. A recording of his explanation would have been very desirable as well as enlightening.

knowledge of him than he is in their going through ritual in attempt to worship him (compare 1 Samuel 15:22-23). This verse also demonstrates that Jehovah, the God of the Old Testament, is a God of mercy as well as justice, something not always understood by readers and teachers of the Old Testament.

Miscellaneous Prophecies

The Lord declares that when Israel was a child (as a nation), he loved him and called him out of Egypt (Hosea 11:1). The house of Israel was in bondage in Egypt until the Lord raised up Moses and called him to lead them back to the land of promise. This, of course, is the similitude of Jesus being in Egypt as a child until the death of Herod (Matthew 2:12-15). At the time of Hosea, Ephraim was seeking an alliance with Egypt. The Lord used this prophecy to teach Ephraim not to return to Egypt but to go into Assyria (Hosea 11:5).

Joseph Smith made only one change in the book of Hosea in his translation of the Bible. However, we should not assume that the rest of the book is intact or correct. The text of Hosea is one of the more corrupt, and apparently Joseph Smith did not have the time to work extensively on it.[40] The change Joseph did make is an important one. It again depicts a message of hope. The Lord's "heart is turned toward (Ephraim), and (his) mercies are extended to gather (her)" (JST Hosea 11:8). In spite of their wickedness, the Lord will not destroy them (Hosea 11:9). He will take them into captivity, scatter them, and later gather them as he has covenanted and as the rest of Hosea testifies. After declaring that Ephraim is not to be destroyed, the Lord again affirms that Judah is still faithful at this time (Hosea 11:12). The Lord then returns to the time of his original covenant with Jacob, the father of Israel.

Using the principle of the resurrection as a teaching symbol,[41] the Lord promises to redeem Ephraim from death that will come upon her (Hosea 13:14). She will be destroyed or die as a nation but will be resur-

---

[40] Sperry, Sidney B. The Voice of Israel's Prophets. Deseret Book, 1952, p. 278.

[41] Hosea 13:14 is similar to 1 Corinthians 15:54-55. Many Bible scholars feel that Paul is quoting or paraphrasing Hosea. While this may be true, another possibility is that both Paul and Hosea are paraphrasing or quoting from an earlier source. The Nephite prophet Abinadi makes reference to the same message and even the same wording as 1 Corinthians 15 in teaching the wicked priests of Noah. He was undoubtedly drawing his information from the plates of brass written before 600 B.C. While the plates probably had Hosea's words on them (see 1 Nephi 5:11-14), the completeness of Abinadi's text suggests another source and Hosea seems to be drawing upon the principle known, not the text or prophecy.

rected or restored. The Lord will destroy her but he also has the power to bring her back and establish her again as a nation. The Lord concludes the chapter with a declaration of desolation upon Samaria, Ephraim's geographic location (Hosea 13:15-16).

Ezekial also used the principle of the resurrection to teach the gathering of Israel. He saw the valley of dry bones coming together, sinews, flesh, skin, and finally putting breath into the restored body. The Lord told Ezekial that these bones represent the whole house of Israel who would come out of their graves (being scattered) and restored to their own lands and come to know the Lord (Ezekial 37:1-14). This prophesy is probably best known from the wonderful old negro spiritual song "the foot bone connected to the ankle bone, the ankle bone connected to the leg bone, etc... now hear the word of the Lord." But unknown to most of those who hear the melody, the message of the restoration of the house of Israel is the word of the Lord that should be heard. The message continues with a prophesy of The Book of Mormon (the stick of Ephraim) coming forth to be put with the Bible (the stick of Judah). It further prophesies of the establishment of the full kingdom of God (Ezekial 37:15-28). A further development of the restoration will come in a later chapter but will be included briefly here.

The last chapter of Hosea ends with an invitation for Israel to return to the Lord through repentance (Hosea 14:1-3). If Israel will accept the invitation, the Lord promises to heal her of her sins and love her freely (Hosea 14:4). In a positive similitude, the Lord compares Israel to a lily whose branches shall spread, whose beauty shall be as the olive tree, and whose smell shall be as Lebanon. Those that dwell under this shadow shall be revived (Hosea 14:5-7). That Ephraim is the chief tribe of this return is shown through the response in Hosea 14:8. Ephraim is to acknowledge that she has forsaken her idols, come unto the Lord, and be restored as his branch.

The prophet Hosea foretold the scattering and gathering of Ephraim, the birthright holder of Israel. While the lily has been planted and the branches have spread much, there is still a lot more growth to come. For those already in the spreading branches or to those who are invited to come and be part of the future growth, the last verse of the book is a fitting conclusion to Hosea's many prophecies of Ephraim. "Who is wise, and he shall understand these things? prudent, and he shall know them? for the ways of the Lord are right, and the just shall walk in them: but the transgressors shall fall therein" (Hosea 14:9).

A New Covenant

Another prophet who spoke specifically of Ephraim is Jeremiah. He gave many prophecies of the restoration of Israel. Of one he said, "in the latter days he shall consider it" (Jeremiah 30:24). The Revised Standard Version of the Bible (hereafter RSV) translates this passage, "in the latter days you shall understand this." This translation reminds us again of Nephi's statement about understanding Isaiah, when his prophecies are fulfilled (2 Nephi 25:7). Jeremiah was referring to what is now Chapter 30 in the book called after him. The chapter speaks of the restoration of Israel and Judah from their scattered condition. We have earlier addressed most of the specifics of these verses. However, the following chapter (31) pertains specifically to Ephraim as the firstborn (v.9) and of the same time as spoken of in the chapter just concluded (30). Wherefore, it will also be understood when it is fulfilled. Several of the verses in Chapter 31, according to Oliver Cowdery, were also quoted by the Angel Moroni to Joseph Smith as soon to be fulfilled (v.6, 8-9; 27-28; 31-33).[42]

The watchmen upon Mount Ephraim will cry, "Arise ye, and let us go up to Zion unto the Lord our God" (31:6). From the verses that follow, this seems to be a prophesy of the Latter-day Saints taking their trek westward to the Rocky Mountains. Since the land of America was given to the house of Joseph (3 Nephi 15:12-13), Mount Ephraim is used to designate the high mountain of America just as was designated the higher mountains in the territory given to Ephraim in the land of Canaan. The following verse (7) foretells an invitation to be given to the chief of the nations (the Gentiles) to gather with the remnant of Israel and obtain salvation. Elder LeGrand Richards interpreted verses 6-14 as a prophecy of the Saints traveling across the plains and settling in the Rocky Mountains.[43]

The Gospel of Matthew quotes Jeremiah 31:15-17 (Matthew 2:16-18) as being fulfilled in part when Rachel (the mother of Joseph and Benjamin) wept for her children because Herod slew all the children of Bethlehem and surrounding areas at the time of the birth of Christ. However, Rachel is further comforted by the prophecy of the restoration

---

[42] Messenger and Advocate, April 1835, pp. 110-111. Oliver Cowdery also said he also quoted 30:18-21. It is interesting that in some of the verses "and the house of Judah" is excluded (31:27) showing a later time for the restoration of Judah. Only the verses that specifically apply to Ephraim will be considered here. For a fuller explanation of both chapters see Monte S. Nyman, The Words of Jeremiah, chapter 12, Bookcraft Inc. S.L.C., 1982.

[43] Richards, LeGrand Marvelous Work and a Wonder, pp.224-228.

of Israel through the firstborn (covenant) son of Joseph, Ephraim. The restoration would constitute a new covenant with the house of Israel and Judah (Jeremiah 31:31-34). The Prophet Joseph explained how this covenant, offered in the Meridian of time, had been rejected but was to be fulfilled in the latter days and was now being fulfilled.[44] Again it is through Ephraim that the covenant was restored. The tribe of Ephraim was the one to return and become the mother trunk to which the branches would be grafted.

A Tenth Shall Return

When Isaiah was called as a prophet, he was told that the cities (of Northern Israel) would be left without inhabitant and the Lord would remove men far away (Isaiah 6:11-12). The 721 B.C. captivity by Assyria fulfilled this prophecy. He then declared: "But yet there shall be a tenth, and they shall return, and shall be eaten, as a teil-tree, and as an oak whose substance is in them when they cast their leaves; so the holy seed shall be the substance thereof" (2 Nephi 16:13; Isaiah 6:13).

The "tenth" that was to return could be interpreted in two ways: a percentage of the people, or one of the ten tribes that would be taken away. Since the number to be gathered was to be many more than previous gatherings (see Deuteronomy 33:17; Isaiah 54:1-3; Jeremiah 16:14-16), it seems more logical that the tenth has reference to one of the tribes. The new Catholic version of the Bible reads, "And there shall be a tithing therein, and she shall return" (Isaiah 6:13). This could suggest one tribe within.

We believe, that the tribe that would be logically and scripturally the one to return would be Ephraim. Ephraim holds the birthright and would thus have the responsibility to care for the other tribes of Israel (Genesis 48:20; 1 Chronicles 5:1-2; Jeremiah 31:9). The gathering of Ephraim first would enable her to fulfill this responsibility. Ephraim being the tribe returning is further substantiated by the gathering that has taken place in this dispensation. In the words of President Joseph F. Smith, "A striking peculiarity of the Saints gathered from all parts of the earth is that they are almost universally of the blood of Ephraim."[45]

Ephraim has been gathered and is the one who will be the instrument in the Lord's hand to gather the other tribes. Those who study Isaiah in light of the latter-day restoration should understand this prophecy.

---

[44] <u>Teachings of the Prophet Joseph Smith</u>, pp. 14-15.
[45] Smith, Joseph F. Gospel Doctrine p. 115.

The tenth being eaten "as a teil tree, and as an oak," (Isaiah 6:13) also has a latter-day connotation. In the marginal note reading of the King James Bible an alternative wording is offered, "when it is returned, and hath been broused." This alternate reading suggests the return will be after Israel has been scattered among the Gentiles and has been purged from the wickedness that caused Israel to be scattered in the first place.

The teil tree and the oak tree are deciduous trees. Each winter they appear to be dead but springtime brings new life. Symbolically this represents the ten tribes who were taken away and were lost or appeared as dead to the world, but when their leaves are spread (among the Gentiles) and when springtime comes (the Restoration), the holy seed (birthright holders) shall be the substance (basis) of a new life. The RSV concludes the verse with "whose stump remains standing when it is felled. The holy seed is its stump" (6:13).

The New King James version renders a similar translation. The felling of the tree is symbolic of the captivity of Israel while the stump, being the holy seed, is a further indication of the birthright concept. The stump would symbolically be the trunk of the tree or the leading tribe. This fits beautifully into Zenos' allegory of the house of Israel and the establishment of the mother trunk into which the rest of the branches of Israel are to be grafted (Jacob 5:52-63). Thus the returning tenth of the house of Israel seems obviously to be Ephraim established as the remnant of Israel in the latter days.

Isaiah prophesied that "in that day (a future day) shall the Lord of Hosts be for a crown of glory, and for a diadem of beauty, unto the residue of his people" (28:5). The previous verses of this chapter was a message of doom to the drunkards of Ephraim (vv.1-4). Therefore, in this context the crown of glory will come upon Ephraim. This interpretation is supported by modern-day revelation (D&C 133:26-34) and will be discussed in a later chapter. Suffice it to say here that the crown of glory is the temple endowment that Ephraim will administer to the rest of the tribes of Israel.

The Psalmist calls Ephraim "the strength of (the Lord's) head" (Psalms 60:7; 108:8). The Psalms (the ancient Israel songbook) are usually based on other scriptures or prophecies. The Psalmist had recognized that Ephraim was the head tribe, the birthright holder to "head" the work of the Lord in the latter days. The analogy of the Psalmist undoubtedly came from the prophecies we have discussed in this chapter and others such as Zechariah saying Ephraim shall be like a mighty man. "I will hiss for them, and gather them; for I have redeemed them: and they shall increase as they have increased. And I will sow them among the people:

and they shall remember me in far countries; and they shall live with their children, and turn again" (Zechariah 10:8-9).

After further describing the gathering of Ephraim, Zechariah tells us what the Lord will do for them. "And I will strengthen them in the LORD; and they shall walk up and down in his name, saith the LORD" (Zechariah 10:12).

CHAPTER 6

Ephraim In The Book of Mormon

There are only seven references in the entire Book of Mormon that mention Ephraim and all of these are from the writings of Isaiah as recorded in the Second Book of Nephi and as copied from the Brass Plates of Laban. Before addressing these specific references pertaining to Ephraim however, we want to place his tribe in a broader context for greater understanding.

Joseph is a Fruitful Bough

To begin with, the Lord's commandments given to return to Jerusalem a second time was to eventually fulfill a blessing given to Joseph by his father Jacob, who was also the father of the twelve tribes of Israel. Jacob had blessed Joseph in the following words, as recorded in Genesis 49: 22 and 26.

Joseph is a fruitful bough, even a fruitful bough by a well; whose branches run over the wall.

The blessings of thy father have prevailed above the blessings of my progenitors unto the utmost bound of the everlasting hills: they shall be on the head of Joseph, and on the crown of the head of him that was separate from his brethren.

Joseph had two sons, Manasseh and Ephraim. Lehi was a descendant of Manasseh (Alma 10: 3), and Ishmael was a descendant of Ephraim. If we didn't know this through modern prophets that Ishmael, whose daughters married the sons of Lehi, was of the tribe of Ephraim, we could come to a misunderstanding that The Book of Mormon was really a record of the tribe of Manasseh. However, Elder Erasmus Snow clarifies,

Whoever has read The Book of Mormon carefully will have learned that the remnants of the house of Joseph dwelt upon the American continent; and that Lehi learned by searching the records of his fathers that were written upon the plates of brass, that he was of the lineage of Manasseh. The Prophet Joseph informed us that the record of Lehi, was contained on the 116 pages that were first translated and subsequently stolen, and of which an abridgement is given us in the first Book of Nephi, which is the record of Nephi individually, he himself being of the lineage of Manasseh; but that Ishmael was of the lineage of Ephraim, and that his sons married into Lehi's family, and Lehi's sons married Ishmael's daughters, thus fulfilling the words of Jacob upon Ephraim and Manasseh in the 48th chapter of Genesis, which says: "And let my name be name on them, and the name of my fathers Abraham and Isaac; and let them grow into a multitude in the midst of the land." Thus these descendants of Manasseh and Ephraim grew together upon this American continent, with a sprinkling from the house of Judah, from Mulek descended, who left Jerusalem eleven years after Lehi, and founded the colony afterwards known as Zarahemla and found by Mosiah—thus making a combination, an intermixture of Ephraim and Manasseh with the remnants of Judah, and for aught we know, the remnants of some other tribes that might have accompanied Mulek. And such have grown up on the American continent.[46]

The Lord, obviously, was involved in getting the two families together—he softened the heart of Ishmael. Both branches of Joseph, Manasseh and Ephraim, were brought to the utmost bounds of the everlasting hills, the Americas and became very fruitful in posterity. Of course, there are many more of the posterity of Joseph who went with the ten tribes into Assyria and the "North." Many of these scattered were among the nations (Amos 9: 8-9) and today are being gathered out of those nations.

The promises made to Joseph and, therefore Ephraim and Manasseh, are great indeed. From 3 Nephi 5: 21-26 we read,

Surely he hath blessed the house of Jacob, and hath been merciful unto the seed of Joseph.

---

[46] Snow, Erasmus. The Journal of Discourses, Vol 23: 184-185.

And insomuch as the children of Lehi have kept his commandments he hath blessed them and prospered them according to his word.

Yea, and surely shall he again bring a remnant of the seed of Joseph to the knowledge of the Lord their God.

And as surely as the Lord liveth, will he gather in from the four quarters of the earth all the remnant of the seed of Jacob, who are scattered abroad upon all the face of the earth.

And as he hath covenanted with all the house of Jacob, even so shall the covenant wherewith he hath covenanted with the house of Jacob be fulfilled in his own due time, unto the restoring all the house of Jacob unto the knowledge of the covenant that he hath covenanted with them.

And then shall they know their Redeemer, who is Jesus Christ, the Son of God; and then shall they be gathered in from the four quarters of the earth unto their own lands, from whence they have been dispersed; yea, as the Lord liveth so shall it be. Amen.

We read further, that the Lord had covenanted with "your father Jacob" that his people would be established in this land (America) "and it shall be a New Jerusalem. And the powers of heaven shall be in the midst of this people; yea, even I will be in the midst of you" (3 Nephi 20:22). The Lord further notes that those who come to this favored land (a land of their inheritance) must be repentant, must hearken to his words and then "they build a city, which shall be called the New Jerusalem" (3 Nephi 21: 22-23; see also Ether 13: 6-10).

Isaiah: Our Source of Information About Ephraim

Because Isaiah is our only source of prophetic information about Ephraim in The Book of Mormon, we feel it important to say a few things about him (Isaiah) before an actual review of the references.

We are fortunate indeed to have the Book of Isaiah for at least two reasons. The first is that we were commanded by the Lord to study Isaiah's writings. For said He,

And now, behold, I say unto you, that ye ought to search these things. Yea, a commandment I give unto you that ye search these things diligently; for great are the words of Isaiah.

> For surely he spake as touching all things concerning my people
> which are of the house of Israel; therefore it must needs be that he
> must speak also to the Gentiles (3 Nephi 23:1-2).

It is obvious, if the Lord commands us to study Isaiah that there is
much for us to learn about the Gospel from it, particularly about the "house
of Israel" and about our Israelite heritage and about events that will
transpire in the future as, perhaps, pertaining to Ephraim's role in the
gathering out from among the Gentiles remnants of the House of Israel.

Secondly, and in connection with the above, Isaiah's teachings represent revelations for our day particularly as they pertain to the covenants
which the Father has made with his people who were scattered "abroad
upon the face of the earth" (3 Nephi 20:12-13) and who will be gathered
from the four corners of the earth in our very day. Isaiah is the definitive
text, when understood, about events which pertain to the Second Coming
of Jesus Christ. It goes without saying, then, that from these writings we
obtain many important revelations about our day—they are loaded with
prophecies for our time.

We think, as well, that there is much for us to learn about Ephraim
from the writings of Isaiah, as we will try to demonstrate shortly.

Isaiah's ministry spanned a period of about twenty years in the
Northern Kingdom of Israel (which incidentally is sometimes called the
Kingdom of Ephraim). In addition, Isaiah preached and prophesied for
about twenty four years in the Southern Kingdom of Judah. In the
Northern Kingdom, he warned the Israelites of their pending doom if
they didn't repent of their iniquities—he warned that the Assyrians
would come to destroy them, to lead them into captivity and that eventually they would be scattered among the nations of the earth. He also
warned the tribe of Judah (Southern Kingdom) of its pending trials and
tribulations if she, too, would not repent.

True to Isaiah's prophecies, the Northern Kingdom was overrun by
Assyrian forces and many of the people were carted away into Assyria
and from there scattered abroad. We know, too, of the captivity of the
Jews by the Babylonians and of their eventual scattering to all corners of
the earth.

Book of Mormon Prophecies Pertaining to Ephraim

It is in the historic setting we have described above that Isaiah prophesied concerning the tribe of Ephraim who were the dominant and powerful
leaders in the Northern Kingdom. In Isaiah's account and obviously prior

to Ephraim's scattering (2 Nephi 17; Isaiah 7), Ephraim entered into an alliance with the Syrians. Apparently, the king of Syria (Rezin) and the king of the Northern Kingdom (Pekah son of Remaliah) "went up toward Jerusalem to war against it, but could not prevail against it" (2 Nephi 17:1). There is a poignant sense here as the house of David was moved by this confederation between the Syrians and Ephraim to make war upon them.

Isaiah was told to meet Ahaz, king of Judah and say unto him: "Take heed, and be quiet; fear not, neither be faint-hearted for the two tails of these smoking firebrands, ...It (the confederacy) "shall not stand, neither shall it come to pass" (2 Nephi 17:3-7).

We sense the mischief that Ephraim was about in these verses. Ephraim seemed to, as a matter of habit, "vex" Judah and was an enemy to righteousness. Ephraim's unrighteousness prompted Isaiah to prophesy that she would "not stand" and "within three score and five years shall Ephraim be broken that it be not a people" (2 Nephi 17:7-8).

History teaches that the Northern Kingdom or Ephraim was actually conquered in 721 or 722 B.C. She was taken to Assyria, along with the other tribes of the Northern Kingdom (ten in all) where they were in bondage and eventually scattered and became "unknown" from that time on. And it is only in our time, that is since the time of the Restoration of the Gospel of Jesus Christ, that there has been, as prophesied, a gathering of these remnants of the House of Israel and, more particularly, the remnants of the House of Ephraim.

It is interesting, as we read further on in this chapter (2 Nephi 17) that the Lord, as prophesied by Isaiah, intended to "shave with a razor that is hired, ...by the king of Assyria, the head, and the hair of the feet; and it shall also consume the beard" (2 Nephi 17:20). This, we believe, has reference to the Lord allowing Assyria to punish Ephraim, to destroy her lands, her vineyards, her flocks and herds because of her wayward behavior. And thus, God brought His judgment to bear on Ephraim, as He often does, by the hand of oppressive rulers. There is the promise, however, that at some future time, Ephraim would be gathered again and eventually enjoy the blessings the Lord had in store for her all along had she been righteous.

Darkness would prevail over Ephraim as she was scattered to all corners of the earth, particularly into the north countries. This, of course, was a foreshadowing of the darkness that, at some time in the future, would cover the earth, even an apostasy prior to the final dispensation of the fullness of times. And just as Ephraim, because of her wickedness brought about the darkness in early times, she would play a part in bringing light to the world after the long and painful time of apostasy.

There is, as often happens, a certain irony in this, even a kind of poetic justice. But, Ephraim, as history will eventually attest, prevailed and in the last days she has arisen from her ignoble past to take a favored place in the work of the last days—in the Restoration of the Gospel of Jesus Christ and in the gathering of the lost tribes of Israel.

In 2 Nephi 19, we have Isaiah's messianic message of hope. It is here that Isaiah predicts that Israel will emerge from darkness into light—it is the light of the Messiah that will eventually cover the earth.

> For unto us a child is born, unto us a son is given; and the government shall be upon his shoulder; and his name shall be called, Wonderful, Counselor, The Mighty God, The Everlasting Father, The Prince of Peace.

> Of the increase of government and peace there is no end, ...and to establish it with judgment and with justice from henceforth, even forever. The zeal of the Lord of Hosts will perform this (2 Nephi 19:6-7).

And of course, Ephraim, as predicted, will play a key role in helping the Lord of Hosts fulfill the final chapter of the great Plan of Salvation as pertaining to this earth. But it will only be after she has repented of "pride and stoutness of heart" (2 Nephi 19:9); has ceased her following after "leaders of this people" who cause them to err (2 Nephi 19:16); repented of her wickedness which "burneth as the fire" (2 Nephi 19:18); ceased neglecting the "fatherless and widows" (2 Nephi 19:17) and put aside her arrogance and evil performed against Judah (2 Nephi 19:21). For all these evils, the Lord's anger "is not turned away, but his hand is stretched out still" to Ephraim and her fellows (2 Nephi 19:21; see also verses 12 and 17). None of God's rebellious and wayward children, at least in a collective way, deserve much of His kindness and mercy, but toward the House of Israel and particularly Ephraim, He holds out patiently, knowing the end from the beginning, the hand of fellowship.

Let the News be Broadcast—Ephraim is on the Lord's Side

Of all of Isaiah's writings, none is of greater interest to Latter-day Saints than the eleventh chapter of Isaiah or 2 Nephi 21. And because it has such significance for the tribe of Ephraim, we will review a major portion of the chapter here.

The chapter begins with a reference to a "rod" which shall "come forth" (2 Nephi 21:1). This rod is the Prophet Joseph Smith, or as noted in D&C 113 the "servant in the hands of Christ who is partly a descendant of Jesse as well as of Ephraim" (D&C 113:4). The rod came out of the "stem of Jesse" which is our Lord and Savior Jesus Christ (D&C 113: 2). In addition, there is a reference to a branch which shall grow out of its (the stem's) roots. This branch is apparently The Church of Jesus Christ of Latter-day Saints established in these the last days.

The Spirit of the Lord, as noted in verse 2, rested on the rod or upon Joseph Smith and gave to him much power, power necessary to translate The Book of Mormon. In addition, from The Book of Mormon, we learn that it is Joseph Smith who will "judge the poor, and reprove with equity for the meek of the earth" (2 Nephi 21:4) And it is The Book of Mormon that shall "smite the earth with the rod of his mouth, and with the breath of his lips shall he slay the wicked." In other words, it is The Book of Mormon that will bring judgment upon the world (Revelations 14:7). Indeed, people will be judged according to The Book of Mormon. From 2 Nephi 25:21-22 we read,

> Wherefore, for this cause hath the Lord God promised unto me that these things which I write shall be kept and preserved, and handed down unto my seed, from generation to generation, that the promise may be fulfilled unto Joseph, that his seed should never perish as long as the earth should stand.

> Wherefore, these things shall go from generation to generation as long as the earth shall stand; and they shall go according to the will and pleasure of God; and the nations who shall possess them shall be judged of them according to the words which are written.

It is easy to see, as we digress a moment from the teachings of Isaiah, that Ephraim clearly has her work cut out in these last days—that is to take The Book of Mormon to the world so that eventually the world will be left without excuse before the judgment bar of God.

Isaiah looked ahead to our time when the Lord

> shall set his hand again the second time to recover the remnant of his people which shall be left, from Assyria, and from Egypt, and from Pathros, and from Cush, and from Elam, and from Shinar, and from Hamath, and from the islands of the sea (2 Nephi 21:11).

The remnants spoken of here are scattered Israel who are to be gathered in from the four corners of the earth to assume their rightful place in the Kingdom of God—Ephraim is to take the lead in this work. As Latter-day Saints know, this work is central to the missionary effort and is going on at the present time with vigor and enthusiasm under the direction of modern prophets. Among Heavenly Father's many miracles being performed throughout the world, the gathering of Israel is most prominent. Here we have the servants of God, who for the most part are Ephraimites and young ones at that, going forth among the nations of the earth declaring the "voice of Jesus Christ" (D&C 29:1) and, miraculously, His "elect hear my voice and harden not their hearts" against it (D&C 29:7). The gathering of Israel, as prophesied by holy prophets from the beginning of time is truly one of the great miracles ever performed on earth.

In addition, the Lord, "...shall set up an ensign for the nations, and shall assemble the outcasts of Israel and gather together the dispersed of Judah from the four corners of the earth (2 Nephi 21:12). We believe that the "ensign" spoken of here is The Book of Mormon and the Church and when this ensign is placed in the hands of faithful Ephraim, as she tries to fulfill her divine destiny, it is a mighty and formidable force to reckon with. Indeed, He, the Lord Jesus Christ, will "smite the earth with the rod of his mouth, and with the breath of his lips shall he slay the wicked" (2 Nephi 21:4). These words mean that the Lord's servant (Joseph Smith) has had the Lord's spirit "rest upon him" (2 Nephi 21:1-2) and has had power given him to translate The Book of Mormon and it is The Book of Mormon that will smite the earth and it (The Book of Mormon) will judge the earth (Revelations 14:6). In other words, it is The Book of Mormon that will be the judge of the world. Hence, the missionaries go about teaching the world about The Book of Mormon and, in this way, "recover the remnant of the his people" (2 Nephi 21:11).

And miracle of all miracles—"The envy of Ephraim also shall depart, and the adversaries of Judah shall be cut off; Ephraim shall not envy Judah, and Judah shall not vex Ephraim" (2 Nephi 21:13). No verse in modern scripture is as poignant as this—the arch enemies of olden times will some day put their arms around each other and weep for joy. They will be friends again, even brothers.

CHAPTER 7

Ephraim In The Doctrine and Covenants

As in The Book of Mormon, there are in the Doctrine and Covenants only a very few references pertaining to Ephraim—only six to be exact and three of those are in one section (D&C 133). We will take the references in order and elaborate on each.

We first turn to Doctrine and Covenants 27. This is a revelation that begins by explaining to the Saints, through the Prophet Joseph Smith, that it "mattereth not what ye shall eat or what ye shall drink when ye partake of the sacrament, if it so be that ye do it with an eye single to my glory…" The revelation is in the form of a warning, that "wine" or "strong drink" should not be purchased from "your enemies."

The Stick of Ephraim

After having given the above warning and instruction pertaining to the sacrament, the Lord speaks of a future great sacrament meeting which will be attended by ancient apostles and prophets. The first prophet he mentions is, as the scripture notes, Moroni.

> Behold, this is wisdom in me; wherefore, marvel not, for the hour cometh that I will drink of the fruit of the vine with you on the earth, and with Moroni, whom I have sent unto you to reveal The Book of Mormon, containing the fulness of my everlasting gospel, to whom I have committed the keys of the record of the stick of Ephraim. (D&C 27:5)

Unto Moroni was committed the "record" of the Stick of Ephraim or The Book of Mormon which contains the fulness of the everlasting gospel. Moroni, of course, in turn committed the record to the Prophet Joseph Smith. The record gives an account "of the former inhabitants of this continent, and the source from whence they sprang" (Joseph Smith—History 1:34). Moroni also delivered other important items to the young prophet:

> Also, that there were two stones in silver bows—and these stones, fastened to a breastplate, constituted what is called the Urim and Thummim—deposited with the plates; and the possession and use of these stones were what constituted "seers" in ancient or former times; and that God had prepared them for the purpose of translating the book. (Joseph Smith—History 1:35)

Although the "stick of Ephraim" is not specifically mentioned in the Joseph Smith account in the Pearl of Great Price, from the revelation in Doctrine and Covenants 27 we learn that the "keys" to this record of the stick of Ephraim were, in fact, given to Joseph Smith.

The Book of Mormon is referred to in the Bible as the "stick of Ephraim" or the "stick of Joseph in the hand of Ephraim" (Ezekiel 37:16-19). The stick of Joseph "which is in the hand of Ephraim" will be joined with the "stick of Judah" (the Bible) and they shall become "one stick, and they shall be one in mine hand." Speaking of this symbolism, Orson Pratt has said,

> it was a symbol of two records; for it is well known that records were kept in ancient times on parchment; rolled upon sticks...All the prophecies of Jeremiah for many years were written and rolled round a stick, and were called a book; so in Ezekiel these sticks represent two records, one the record of the tribe of Joseph, and the other of Judah[47]

As Elder Bruce R. McConkie explained, The Book of Mormon is a record of God's dealings with the tribe of Ephraim,

> it is the stick of Joseph in the hands of Ephraim in that it records God's dealings with a portion of the tribe of Joseph, the record of which came forth by way of latter-day Ephraim and is now in the hands of church members who nearly all are of Ephraim. (D&C 27:5)[48]

Elder McConkie's point is, in part, based on Lehi's words to his son Joseph as recorded in 2 Nephi 3:11-12. Lehi said,

---

[47] McConkie, Bruce, R. <u>Mormon Doctrine</u>, p. 767.
[48] <u>Ibid.</u>, p. 767.

But a seer will I raise up out of the fruit of thy loins; and unto him will I give power to bring forth my word unto the seed of thy loins— and not to the bringing forth my word only, saith the Lord, but to the convincing them of my word, which shall have already gone forth among them.

Wherefore, the fruit of thy loins shall write; and the fruit of the loins of Judah shall write; and that which shall be written by the fruit of thy loins, and also that which shall be written by the fruit of the loins of Judah, shall grow together, unto the confounding of false doctrines and laying down of contentions, and establishing peace among the fruit of thy loins, and bringing them to the knowledge of their fathers in the latter days, and also to the knowledge of my covenants, saith the Lord.

We next turn to Doctrine and Covenants 64 for another interesting contemplation concerning Ephraim. This is a revelation given to the Prophet Joseph Smith at Kirtland, Ohio dated September 11, 1831. The revelation begins with a warning to a few of the brethren of the early Church to repent of their sins and particularly their sin of accusation against the Prophet Joseph Smith. "There are those who have sought occasion against him without cause" (verse 6). The Lord then declared that Joseph had indeed sinned, but that he had been forgiven—that each of the brethren must forgive him also or stand condemned. The wonderful verse which follows, "I, the Lord, will forgive whom I will forgive, but of you it is required to forgive all men" (v.10) has become a well-known classic in the mental quivers of faithful Latter-day Saints.

Ephraim, Does Not Have Rebellious Blood

Then, after a number of specific calls to repentance and a number of specific assignments, we find in this section these sobering and instructive words,

Behold, the Lord requireth the heart and a willing mind; and the willing and obedient shall eat the good of the land of Zion in these last days.[49]

---

[49] The thirty-fourth verse is almost a verbatim quote of Isaiah 1:19 showing that Isaiah was speaking of the latter-day restoration. One of the purposes of the Doctrine and Covenants was "that it might be fulfilled, which was written by the prophets" (D&C 1:18). The quoting of Isaiah in this revelation is one of many Old or New Testament quotations within the Doctrine and Covenants.

And the rebellious shall be cut off out of the land of Zion, and shall be sent away, and shall not inherit the land.

For, verily I say that the rebellious are not of the blood of Ephraim, wherefore they shall be plucked out. (D&C 64:34-36)

The Lord gave a similar warning to the church members of Rome through his servant Paul (Romans 9: 4-6).

Who are Israelites; to whom pertaineth the adoption, and the glory, and the covenants, and the giving of the law, and the service of God, and the promises;

Whose are the fathers, and of whom as concerning the flesh Christ came, who is over all, God blessed for ever. Amen

Not as though the word of God hath taken none effect. For they are not all Israel, which are of Israel:

Those who rebelled against the Lord and his Church would no longer be a part of his gathered people. In other words, from the revelation given to the Prophet Joseph Smith and from the writings of Paul (both quoted above), we come to understand that the gathering of the blood of Israel from among the Gentiles is a serious matter, whether in Paul's day (Israel gathered out from the Gentile Romans) or the people gather from the Gentiles in our day.

Most, if not all people who enter the waters of baptism and have become converted to the Gospel of Jesus Christ will be of the House of Israel, having in their veins the literal blood, to a greater or lesser degree, of the particular tribes to which they belong. In other words, if you are of the tribe of Manasseh, you will have some literal blood of the tribe of Manasseh in your veins; likewise if you are of the tribe of Dan, you will have some literal blood of the tribe of Dan, and so forth.

In the case of latter-day Ephraim, the gathered members of The Church of Jesus Christ of Latter-day Saints have the literal blood of Ephraim coursing through their veins. In other words, those of us who are of the tribe of Ephraim have Ephraim blood in us.

And this is special blood. All of us of the House of Israel have what might be called "believing blood"[50] in our veins as is implied in this

---

[50] For a more complete treatise on "the believing blood" of the House of Israel, see McConkie, Bruce R. A New Witness for the Articles of Faith, Deseret Book Company, Salt Lake City, Utah 1985, Chapter 4.

section of the Doctrine and Covenants. In the case of Ephraim, it is clear that Ephraim in our time is not rebellious as were they in times of old. It was the tribe of Ephraim, please remember, who rejected the God of Israel in early times and, as a consequence, was driven and scattered by the Assyrians and eventually, Ephraim along with nine other tribes, were soon lost.

In Paul's day, he warned the church members that being of the blood of Israel was not sufficient to save them. They must be doers of the word as well (Romans 2: 6-13). Also, the rebellious gathered Ephraimites in 1837 were cut off out of the land of Zion. They were driven out of Missouri and Ephraim was told they must "wait for a little season for the redemption of Zion" (D&C 105:9).

But Ephraim, for the most part, is now being found. These remnants of the former tribe are hearing the word of God being declared in divers places scattered all over the earth. And, what is terribly important for our purposes here, is that Ephraim is not now rebellious—on the contrary, it is Ephraim who is shouldering the major part of the establishment of Zion in these last days.

We should note briefly here that it is possible to be a member of The Church of Jesus Christ of Latter-day Saints and not have the blood of Israel in his or her veins. If it does happen, however, this person will be adopted into the House of Israel, will have a blood change via the Holy Ghost, and assigned to a tribe, likely the tribe of Ephraim. The Prophet Joseph Smith taught,

It [the Holy Ghost] is more powerful in expanding the mind, enlightening the understanding, and storing the intellect with present knowledge, of a man who is of the literal seed of Abraham, than one that is a Gentile, though it may not have half as much visible effect upon the body; for as the Holy Ghost falls upon one of the literal seed of Abraham, it is calm and serene; and his whole soul and body are only exercised by the pure spirit of intelligence; while the effect of the Holy Ghost upon a Gentile, is to purge out the old blood, and make him actually of the seed of Abraham. That man that has none of the blood of Abraham (naturally) must have a new creation by the Holy Ghost. In such a case, there may be more of a powerful effect upon the body, and visible to the eye, than upon an Israelite, while the Israelite at first might be far before the Gentile in pure intelligence.[51]

---

[51] <u>Teachings of the Prophet Joseph Smith</u>, The Deseret News Press, 1938 edition. Pages 149-150.

Ephraim, Sitteth As A Judge

There is another idea presented in this section of the Doctrine and Covenants that pertains to Ephraim. The next verses which follow those we have quoted above read,

> Behold, I, the Lord, have made my church in these last days like unto a judge sitting on a hill, or in a high place, to judge the nations.

> For it shall come to pass that the inhabitants of Zion shall judge all things pertaining to Zion (D&C 64:37-38).

As we have declared throughout this book, much responsibility has been placed on Ephraim for the building of the Kingdom of God on earth. In addition, it is quite obvious that Ephraim will have much to do pertaining to the judgment of the earth. It is the Church or Ephraim who will sit "on a hill" in judgment in "these last days" to judge the nations of the world. Ephraim will not be the "chief" judge—only the Lord God of Israel can assume that rightful place—but surely Ephraim (particularly the prophets, seers and revelators) will play a prominent part in the judgment. In truth, the judgment won't be all that difficult, for the "ensign" (v.42) has already been established and it is the ensign (in this case ensign refers to Zion or to the Church) that is the standard against which people will, for the most part, judge themselves. There is a law, there is a standard or an ensign, there is the record—all of these things make the judgment pretty self-obvious—maybe even quite easy. Jacob sustains this concept of judgment,

> Wherefore, we shall have a perfect knowledge of all our guilt, and our uncleanness, and our nakedness; and the righteous shall have a perfect knowledge of their enjoyment, and their righteousness, being clothed with purity, yea, even with the robe of righteousness.

> And it shall come to pass that when all men shall have passed from this first death unto life, insomuch as they have become immortal, they must appear before the judgment-seat of the Holy One of Israel; and then cometh the judgment, and then must they be judged according to the holy judgment of God (2 Nephi 9:14-15).

Joseph Smith: Descendant of Joseph and Judah

Doctrine and Covenants section 113 gives us further understanding about Ephraim. We have already discussed this section in the previous chapter where we analyzed part of the eleventh chapter of Isaiah. However, perhaps a further, but brief discussion, is in order here.

In this section, the Prophet Joseph Smith answers important questions from the writings of Isaiah. The second question is of concern to us here. It is, "What is the rod spoken of in the first verse of the 11th chapter of Isaiah, that should come of the Stem of Jesse" (D&C 113:3)?

> Behold, thus saith the Lord: It is a servant in the hands of Christ, who is partly a descendant of Jesse as well as of Ephraim, or of the house of Joseph, on whom there is laid much power. (D&C 113:4)

We have already noted that the "rod" spoken of here is the Prophet Joseph Smith who, we are told in this verse, is a descendant of Jesse (the House of Judah) as well as of Ephraim (or sometimes referred to as the House of Joseph). Therefore, Joseph Smith had both the literal blood of Judah and the literal blood of Ephraim in his veins.[52] This, of course, is terribly important since upon Joseph Smith fell the responsibility to both set up an earthly government, the responsibility of Judah, which will be governed by the "law" and a ministry, the responsibility of Ephraim, from which would go forth the "word" of God. In both respects, he was ably suited and was given "much power" and the keys of the Kingdom and the priesthood rightly belonged to him by lineage (Doctrine and Covenants 113: 6; 90:2-4). Joseph is verified twice in this section as a literal descendant of the ancient patriarchs. We should note also, according to this verse, that Ephraim was a descendant of Joseph, the same Joseph who was the first born of Rachel the wonderful and favored wife of Jacob (Israel). Joseph, we remember, gave his birthright (as one of the twelve sons of Jacob) to his two sons: Ephraim and Manasseh, and it was Jacob who, in a grandfather's blessing, gave the privilege of "first born" to Ephraim.

---

[52] The statement by Brigham Young that Joseph Smith was a "pure Ephraimite" does not necessarily mean he had only the blood of Ephraim in his veins. The above statement shows that he had the pure or literal blood of Judah as well. Since Israel lived among the Gentiles for hundreds of years, it is also possible that the blood of many other tribes or nationalities could have come in through intermarriage.

Treasures Unto Ephraim

Now we turn to perhaps the most intriguing section in the Doctrine and Covenants pertaining to Ephraim—Section 133. This section begins with a warning to the Saints of God to prepare for the Second Coming of Christ. The Saints were admonished to "sanctify yourselves" (v.4) by going out from Babylon. "Be ye clean that bear the vessels of the Lord" (v.5). In addition, the Saints were to go forth "unto the nations which are afar off; unto the islands of the sea; send forth unto foreign lands; call upon all nations, first upon the Gentiles, and then upon the Jews" (vs.8-9). The warning to all nations is emphasized here to repent, to prepare for his coming.

His voice shall be heard everywhere—it shall be uttered out of Zion, and "he shall speak from Jerusalem, and his voice shall be heard among all people" (v.21).

He shall command the great deep, and it shall be driven back into the north countries, and the islands shall become one land;

And the land of Jerusalem and the land of Zion shall be turned back into their own place, and the earth shall be like as it was in the days before it was divided. (vs.23-24)

Then, when all is ready, the Ten Tribes, those who were lost in the "north countries," will come in "remembrance before the Lord" and "their prophets shall hear his voice, and shall no longer stay themselves"(v.26). In other words, when the temple in Jackson County is prepared, those people, who were a part of the scattered remnants of Israel—who were scattered into the north countries, will make haste to reach their objective—the holy temple of the Lord. These are the lost tribes, whether literally or figuratively, we will know when the prophecy is fulfilled (2 Nephi 25:7), who shall "smite the rocks, and the ice shall flow down at their presence" and their enemies shall become a "prey unto them" (v.26).

They will march forth on a great highway which will be cast up for them. They will be so determined that those who are set on thwarting their progress will be overrun and become like a "prey unto them." They will move with frightening power as a formidable force insomuch that the "boundaries of the everlasting hills shall tremble at their presence" (v.31). Those who stand in their way will be trodden down and destroyed. Nothing, in other words, will deter them or stop them from achieving their desire—to receive their endowments and sealings in the holy House of the Lord.

When they arrive in Jackson County, they will be met by a living prophet, the only authorized authority on earth with the keys to assist them with their temple work. Under the direction of the prophet, the satisfying work will begin. With tears of gratitude, Ephraim will embrace these nomads from the north and welcome them into The Church of Jesus Christ of Latter-day Saints, even the Kingdom of God on earth.

These people will bring with them their "rich treasures" (v.30) and present them "unto the children of Ephraim, my servants." These rich treasures won't be any different than the rich treasures that all Latter-day Saints cherish—their genealogical records (among other things) that they have kept for this special moment of sealing (D&C 128: 24). And Ephraim will know what to do with these records—they will have plenty of experience in temple work and will accomplish this work with vigor and enthusiasm.

"And there shall they fall down and be crowned with glory, even in Zion, by the hands of the servants of the Lord, even the children of Ephraim" (D&C 133:32). It will be a glorious moment in the history of the world, when these people will be sealed up unto glory in the celestial courts on high. They will take their place with all righteous saints of God and will realize the promises made to their fathers, even Abraham and Isaac and Jacob. And indeed, "they shall be filled with songs of everlasting joy" (v.33).

For Ephraim, the blessing for all her arduous work in these last days, will finally be manifest. All the suffering of the saints of God at the hands of wicked men, in a very wicked world, will be forgotten—the pain and suffering at Liberty Jail, the unprovoked murder at Hauns Mill, the martyrdom at Carthage, the brutal expulsion from Nauvoo, and the trek of tears across the broad plains—all will be forgotten in the countdown to the triumphant return of our Lord and Savior Jesus Christ.

"Behold, this is the blessing of the everlasting God upon the tribes of Israel, and the richer blessing upon the head of Ephraim and his fellows" (D&C 133:34). While we have maintained throughout this book that great blessings are in store for Ephraim, we must note that these blessings are closely linked with the responsibilities placed upon the head of Ephraim. As President Joseph Fielding Smith has said,

> the members of the Church, most of us of the tribe of Ephraim, are of the remnant of Jacob. We know it to be the fact that the Lord called upon the descendants of Ephraim to commence his work in

the earth in these last days. We know further that he has said that he set Ephraim, according to the promises of his birthright, at the head. Ephraim receives the "richer blessings." these blessings being those of presidency or direction. The keys are with Ephraim. It is Ephraim who is to be endowed with power to bless and give to the other tribes, including the Lamanites, their blessings. All the other tribes of Jacob, including the Lamanites, are to be crowned with glory in Zion by the hands of Ephraim.[53]

---

[53] Smith, Joseph Fielding, Doctrines of Salvation, Volume II, pp. 250-251.

CHAPTER 8

Ephraim to be Opposed in the Latter-days

In the pre-earth life when Lucifer attempted to overthrow the plan of Heavenly Father (Moses 4:1-4), he was expelled from heaven by an army of righteous spirits whose General was the great Jehovah (Moses 4:3) and whose captain was Michael, the archangel (Revelations 12:7). Losing his status as "a son of the morning" (Isaiah 14:12 and D&C 76:26-27), he became the devil (Moses 4:4 and D&C 29:37) destined to become miserable forever. "And because he had fallen from heaven, and had become miserable forever, he sought also the misery of all mankind" (2 Nephi 2:18).

It stands to reason that he would attempt to destroy those who have the greatest potential for resisting him and his evil ways. As discussed earlier, those would be the children of Ephraim. Since God has promised the greater blessings to Ephraim and has given him the commission to prepare the earth for the Second Coming of Christ, it would be naive and unrealistic to believe that Satan would allow the great work of the latter days to roll on unopposed.

While it is true that Satan is interested in the destruction of all mankind, it is equally true that he has his priority list of those who are to be singled out to receive the greatest trials. Note the difference in intensity in the words used to describe how Satan operates regarding the temptations of mankind in general and his demonic "super" efforts against the Latter-day Saint warriors. The Lord revealed to the Prophet Joseph Smith,

And it must needs be that the devil should tempt the children of men, or they could not be agents unto themselves; for if they never should have bitter they could not know the sweet. (D&C 29:39)

He Maketh War with the Saints of God

To the rank and file of humanity, the devil merely "tempts" them. Perhaps that is all that is necessary to gain temporary control over them. However, to the Saints—the great majority of whom are of the tribe of Ephraim, the Lord revealed,

> And while we were yet in the Spirit, the Lord commanded us that we should write the vision; for we beheld Satan, that old serpent, even the devil, who rebelled against God, and sought to take the kingdom of our God and his Christ—

> Wherefore, he maketh war with the saints of God, and encompasseth them round about. (D&C 76:28-29)

It almost seems unfair to be charged with the responsibility to take the gospel to the world, and in turn have Satan focus his greatest destructive power on us. However, President Brigham Young put the trials faced by Latter-day Saints as compared to others in proper perspective.

> I ask, is there a reason for men and women being exposed more constantly and more powerfully, to the power of the enemy, by having visions than by not having them? There is and it is simply this—God never bestows upon His people, or upon an individual, superior blessings without a severe trial to prove them, to prove that individual, or that people to see whether they will keep their covenants with him, and keep in remembrance what He has shown them. Then the greater the vision, the greater the display of the power of the enemy. And when such individuals are off their guard they are left to themselves, as Jesus was. For this express purpose the Father withdrew His spirit from His Son, at the time he was to be crucified. Jesus had been with his Father, talked with Him, dwelt in His bosom, and knew all about heaven, about making the earth, about the transgression of man, and what would redeem the people, and that he was the character who was to redeem the sons of earth, and the earth itself from all sin that had come upon it. The light, knowledge, power, and glory with which he was clothed were far above, or exceeded that of all others who had been upon the earth after the fall, consequently at the very moment, at the hour when the crisis came for him to offer up his life, the Father withdrew Himself, withdrew His Spirit, and cast a veil over him. That is what made him sweat blood. If he

had had the power of God upon him, he would not have sweat blood; but all was withdrawn from him, and a veil was cast over him, and he then plead with the Father not to forsake him. "No," says the Father, "You must have your trials, as well as others."***So when individuals are blessed with visions, revelations, and great manifestations, look out, then the devil is nigh you, and you will be tempted in proportion to the vision, revelation, or manifestation you have received. Hence thousands, when they are off their guard, give way to the severe temptations which come upon them, and behold they are gone.[54]

Missionary Work—The Crucial Barometer of Ephraim's Faithfulness

Well, we might ask, "How is modern Ephraim doing in resisting temptation and fulfilling all that is required of him?" From one vantage point, it seems apparent that Satan is having considerable success in diverting our attention from our foreordained mission. In spite of urgent and pleading calls from modern day prophets, for example, many of these valiant pre-mortal warriors seem to have lost heart for the battle. In fact, in the United States and Canada, only one of every three young men between ages nineteen and twenty-six who are members of the Church, accept the call to serve as missionaries. If the pool of potential missionaries is broadened to include all Latter-day Saint young men everywhere, only one in four rises to accept a call to serve.

Armed with an understanding given by latter-day prophets, are we doing all we can to prepare ourselves for the battle we inevitably must face? Even though the adversary is not wise, we must respect his power to influence us. He is a formidable opponent, indeed. As we can see, compared to the number of people in the world (approximately five and a half billion), how many missionaries are there? At present there are approximately 60,000 missionaries scattered across the globe. The ratio is **one** missionary for every 110,000 people! Who would you focus on if you were the destroyer? When a young missionary goes into the mission field without knowing either who he or she really is (a chosen, foreordained minister of God) or what the opposition that must be faced, is it any wonder that so many of them get blind-sided by the adversary and lose sight of what they should be about? Parents and leaders of the youth must respond more vigorously to President Kimball's challenge to prepare more and to prepare better for the battle.

---

[54] Brigham Young, <u>Journal of Discourses</u> 3:205-206

How can it be that so many of our young people particularly, the noble and great ones from the beginning of time, lose sight of the greater vision and refuse to take the saving gospel to their fellows here on earth? It is obvious that the Adversary has unleashed his "big guns" on the young men and young women of the Church. His tactic, according to Doctrine and Covenants 76:29, is to "encompass them round about." There is not a trick he does not employ; not a tactic he does not use; not a method of destruction he does not implement in attempting to divert these modern warriors away from joining the battle.

Numbers of missionaries alone are not an indication of success. The quality expected of these valiant servants must also be considered. These sons of Ephraim need to be well prepared and dedicated. President Spencer W. Kimball, in extending a challenge to priesthood leaders for more missionaries said that he was not asking for "more scrubs or mentally disturbed missionaries," nor was he asking for those who do not have testimonies or those who are not morally clean. He urged the Latter-day Saints to raise up strong and faithful missionaries from every branch and ward in the Church. He added that young missionaries should come to understand, "that it is a great privilege to go on a mission and that they must be physically well, mentally well, spiritually well, and that "the Lord cannot look upon sin with the least degree of allowance."[55]

Satan's efforts are not limited to the youth. In recent years Church leaders have asked for senior couples to serve Church missions. What lifetime members, living in the heartlands of the Church take for granted, is absolutely revelatory for new members. Although the enthusiasm among new members is difficult to match, without the wisdom of age and experience, many wander into forbidden paths and are lost. How are these seasoned warriors (senior couples) responding to the prophetic call to serve? About one-fifth of the requests for senior couples is currently being filled! Many of those senior couples who serve missions are going for the second, third, fourth, and even fifth time, while the majority refuse to respond at all.

Excuses on why not serve are as many and varied as there are couples. No matter what the reason for refusing to serve a mission, however, the results are still the same—a critical need is left unfilled. There are fears in the hearts of the senior couples that they "don't know enough," that "they can't keep pace with the young missionaries," that "they can't learn a new language in their old age," that "they won't be able to get

---

[55] Spencer W. Kimball, Regional Representative Seminar, April 4, 1974

along with each other for that length of time" and on *ad infinitum*. Perhaps we have forgotten Saint Paul's stirring charge: "For God hath not given us the spirit of fear; but of power, and of love, and of a sound mind" (2 Timothy 1:7). What of Nephi's bold declaration:

> I will go and do the things which the Lord hath commanded, for I know that the Lord giveth no commandments unto the children of men, save he shall prepare a way for them that they may accomplish the thing which he commandeth them (1 Nephi 3:7).

Satan's Kingdom In Opposition to God's

As the gospel continues to spread across the face of the globe, we can expect that the power of the Adversary will increase proportionately. The Prophet Joseph Smith said, In relation to the kingdom of God, the devil always sets up his kingdom at the very same time in opposition to God.[56]

Without the spirit of despair or gloom, our Church leaders have continued to encouraged us to do better even in the face of the opposition—to try harder to carry off triumphant the Kingdom of God, to come up to the status we earned in the pre-earth life. Patriarch Hyrum G. Smith said in a general conference,

> I regret that there are many among us who are not as loyal as we should like to have them. It grieves me and it grieves my co-laborers, and I am sure it grieves the Lord, when word comes that our fellows have been untrue to trusts imposed upon them or in them; and we, every one of us, know that it is wrong when we are untrue to a trust, or break a sacred confidence...
>
> When any of us are caught in the snares of temptation and fall by the wayside, it not only hurts us individually but it hurts all of us... We are only a few in number compared to the great host in the world, and we must remember and know that where the Lord requires responsibility, he expects us to be loyal and true to it. Therefore the responsibility is upon our shoulders as gathered Ephraim, living here in the land of Ephraim, in the tops of the mountains, in the midst of the everlasting hills, where the Lord has selected a gathering place and named it through the mouths of his holy prophets, both ancient

---

[56] Teachings of the Prophet Joseph Smith, Section Six 1843-44 p.365

and modern. "This is the place," and here it will be required at our hands, not only by our words but by our every day conduct.[57]

Even though many people seem to have lost the vision of who they are and why they are privileged to live in this day, the Lord has not given up on helping us all learn what we need to learn even even if it is by the things that we suffer. President Joseph Fielding Smith said,

> Even as it was it took years of training and constant guidance on the part of divinely appointed prophets to impress upon the people the sacredness of their special call. Moreover, they had to suffer for the transgression of the law and the breaking of covenants, be whipped and suffer bondage before they could learn their lesson.[58]

Although we won't explore the nature of suffering here, the Lord gave us the key to withstanding the trials and temptations which the Adversary puts in our paths in his devilish attempt to thwart His work. Through the Apostle Paul (Ephesians 6:11-18) and also through the Prophet Joseph Smith, the Lord urged us to put on the whole armor of God that we may be able to firmly stand in the evil hour preceding the Second Coming of the Savior:

> Wherefore, lift up your hearts and rejoice, and gird up your loins, and take upon you my whole armor, that ye may be able to withstand the evil day, having done all, that ye may be able to stand.
>
> Stand, therefore, having your loins girt about with truth, having on the breastplate of righteousness, and your feet shod with the preparation of the gospel of peace, which I have sent mine angels to commit unto you;
>
> Taking the shield of faith wherewith ye shall be able to quench all the fiery darts of the wicked;
>
> And take the helmet of salvation, and the sword of my Spirit, which I will pour out upon you, and my word which I reveal unto you, and be agreed as touching all things whatsoever ye ask of me, and be

---

[57] Hyrum G. Smith, Conference Report, April 1923, p.98
[58] Joseph Fielding Smith Jr., The Way to Perfection, p.130

faithful until I come, and ye shall be caught up, that where I am ye shall be also. Amen (D&C 27:15-18).

Whether in our personal or family life, in our neighborhood associations, or even in our Church lives, we need to expect opposition from the Adversary. Perhaps the intensity of that opposition is a signal as to how worried he is about our potential harm to his worldly kingdom. We are promised that if we do all we can, we will be able to stand in the evil day.

CHAPTER 9

Go Forth My Sons [Ephraim] and Find The Lost Sheep of the House of Israel

The prophets have eloquently spoken of the responsibility of Ephraim to teach the Gospel to all of Father's children. Brigham Young, for example, said,

> It is Ephraim that I have been searching for all the days of my preaching, and that is the blood which ran in my veins when I embraced the Gospel. If there are any of the other tribes mixed with the Gentiles we are also searching for them.[59]

Elders to Hunt Them From the Hills

Still the task seems impossible to find so few among the teeming billions on the face of the earth. And so it would have been, except that the great God of Heaven intervened and put into the heart of the sons and daughters of Ephraim the desire to find the truth rather than to wait for the truth to find them. Elder Erastus Snow described the spirit that moves people to "hunt for the elders."

> And it is the foremost of those spirits whom the Lord has prepared to receive the Gospel when it was presented to them, and who did not wait for the Elders to hunt them from the hills and corners of the earth, but they were hunting for the Elders, impelled by a spirit which then they could not understand; and for this reason were they among the first Elders of the Church; they and the fathers having

---

[59] Brigham Young quoted by Joseph Fielding Smith Jr., The Way to Perfection, p.128

been watched over from the days that God promised those blessings upon Isaac and Jacob and Joseph and Ephraim. And these are they that will be found in the front ranks of all that is noble and good in their day and time, and who will be found among those whose efforts are directed in establishing upon the earth those heaven-born principles which tend directly to blessing and salvation, to ameliorating the condition of their fellow-men, and elevating them in the scale of their being; and among those also who receive the fullness of the Everlasting Gospel, and the keys of Priesthood in the last days, through whom God determined to gather up again unto himself a peculiar people, a holy nation, a pure seed that shall stand upon Mount Zion as saviors, not only to the house of Israel but also to the house of Esau.[60]

This process of gathering from amidst the masses was clearly taught during the early days of the restoration. After thoroughly (and prophetically) searching the Bible, Brigham Young inquired,

But where is the stick of Joseph? Can you tell where it is? Yes. It was the children of Joseph who came across the waters to this continent, and this land was filled with people, and The Book of Mormon or the stick of Joseph contains their writings, and they are in the hands of Ephraim. Where are the Ephraimites? They are mixed through all the nations of the earth. God is calling upon them to gather out, and he is uniting them, and they are giving the Gospel to all the world. Is there any harm or any false doctrine in that? A great many say there is. If there is, it is all in the Bible.[61]

Ephraim Blankets the Earth with Missionaries

How could an impoverished people like the Latter-day Saints who were forced to flee their homes and belongings in New York, Ohio, Missouri, and finally Illinois, ever amass sufficient resources to enable them to blanket the earth with missionaries? New light was shed on the answer to that question by apostle Melvin J. Ballard.

I was deeply impressed with the statement made not long since by a man who has been gathering statistics of an eminent character,

---

[60] Journal of Discourses, Vol.23, pp.185-186, Erastus Snow, May 6, 1882
[61] Discourses of Brigham Young, p.127, Journal of Discourses 13:174

wherein he calls attention to the fact that while the United States is but seven percent of the world's land, and has but six percent of the world's population, nearly one-half of the world's natural wealth is in the United States of America. This surely is a choice land above all other lands. And then, as I thought of our habitations in these mountains, I feel a confidence in the statement that taking a survey two hundred miles from this city in either direction, and circumscribing a district within that radius, there may be found more natural wealth than in any other like territory in any other portion of this choice land. We are not only in the right nation, we are in the right part of that nation.[62]

Continuing the theme of the Lord providing resources for Ephraim to accomplish his foreordained task. Rulon S. Wells said, "Under the new and everlasting covenant the Lord has made land grants to his chosen people.[63]

One would think that with a task of this magnitude to perform, the God of the Heavens would send His very strongest children to the forefront. And so He has, but not strong as to academic standards, or physical and mental stature, the Lord's latter-day missionary force is not overwhelming to the worldly or those who lack the vision to see the hand of God working among the nations. Even as the Lord described them, one gets the impression that the Lord does not want people converted to the messengers but to the message. The Gospel is not to be preached with personality and charisma but by the power of the Holy Spirit.

Wherefore, I call upon the weak things of the world, those who are unlearned and despised, to thrash the nations by the power of my Spirit;

And their arm shall be my arm, and I will be their shield and their buckler; and I will gird up their loins, and they shall fight manfully for me; and their enemies shall be under their feet; and I will let fall the sword in their behalf, and by the fire of mine indignation will I preserve them. (D&C 35:13-14)

Words like **weak, unlearned** and **despised** are often applied to missionaries and could be interpreted as condescending excepting that they

---

[62] Melvin J. Ballard, Conference Report, October 1924, p.29
[63] Rulon S. Wells, Conference Report, October 1939, p.112

were used by the Lord who never lies and never makes a mistake. Why would He send such servants to do His bidding? He answered this question, "to thrash the nations by the power of my Spirit."

The Lord trumpets the same theme with even more power later when He assures missionaries that they will not walk alone but rather be guided by his protecting hand. If they will be faithful, they "shall not be weary in mind, neither darkened, neither in body, limb, nor joint; and a hair of his head shall not fall to the ground unnoticed. And they shall not go hungry, neither athirst" (D&C 84:80).

> And whoso receiveth you, there I will be also, for I will go before your face. I will be on your right hand and on your left, and my Spirit shall be in your hearts, and mine angels round about you, to bear you up. (D&C 84:88)

One wonders if the missionaries of these latter-days recognize the power they have and the closeness of the association they enjoy with the Spirit, angels, and the Savior himself. Is it then any wonder that the Lord confidently proclaimed: "Verily, thus saith the Lord unto you—there is no weapon that is formed against you shall prosper" (D&C 71:9).

The Father Has Not Forgotten His Chosen People

When one stands back from the mass of material which has been written and spoken about the spreading of the gospel during this final dispensation, it becomes evident that what is happening now is not by chance. Heaven and earth have joined hands in this monumental work. However, the Gospel was not designed solely for the temporal and spiritual benefit of Ephraim. What of the other eleven Tribes of Israel. In 1938 Harold W. Pratt commenting on a thought sparked by Melvin J. Ballard said,

> Brother Ballard, in his talk, drew our attention to the fact that we are of Israel, that we have been gathered out from among the nations of the earth for a glorious purpose, to serve as a city set upon a hill, and to guide those who are honest in heart through this perilous revolutionary period. He has told us that we are charged with taking the Gospel to that remnant of the House of Israel who are not of Ephraim.[64]

---

64 Harold W. Pratt, <u>Conference Report</u>, April 1938, p.116

Even beyond the scope of the work that is now being done in searching out scattered Israel, there is even more than meets the eye. The Father has not forgotten His chosen children from whatever tribe they may have descended. Joseph Fielding Smith summarizes the Prophet Joseph Smith's and Brigham Young's teachings when he said,

> The Prophet Joseph Smith looked forward to the great day when Israel would be gathered. He stated at a conference of the Church held in June, 1831, "that John the Revelator was then among the ten tribes of Israel who had been led away by Shalmaneser, king of Assyria, to prepare them for their return from their long dispersion." President Young frequently had similar thoughts in mind and expressed them. Another of his remarks includes the following: "It is the House of Israel, we are after * * * and it is the very lad on whom father Jacob laid his hands, that will save the House of Israel. The Book of Mormon came to Ephraim, for Joseph Smith was a pure Ephraimite."[65]

Ephraim to be Gathered First

It was not coincidental that the descendants of Ephraim were chosen and assigned in pre-earth life to first gather their fellow Ephraimites to the gospel here in mortality, and then to seek out their brothers and sisters from the other tribes. Would it be a surprise then, that Joseph Smith, the Prophet, was designated as a "pure Ephramite?" Commenting further on the sequence of the gathering, President Joseph Fielding Smith has written,

> Ephraim must be gathered first to prepare the way through the gospel and the priesthood, for the rest of the tribes of Israel when the time comes for them to be gathered to Zion. The great majority of those who have come into the Church are Ephraimites. It is the exception to find one of any other tribe, unless it is of Manasseh...[66]

If a Latter-day Saint does not go on a full time mission, is he or she excluded from participating in the great gathering scene? President Wilford Woodruff placed emphasis on the essential nature of every part of the preparing and gathering process. He said,

---

[65] Joseph Fielding Smith Jr., The Way to Perfection, p.127-128
[66] Joseph Fielding Smith Jr., Doctrines of Salvation, Vol.3, p.252

One of the most important and responsible fields of labor in Zion is that committed to the care of those who preside over and teach in the primaries, Sabbath schools, and Improvement associations, and those who are teaching private day schools among the Latter-day Saints. Who can comprehend the result of the labor performed by the elders of Israel in these branches? No man, unless filled with the revelations of heaven and the inspiration of Almighty God. We send out hundreds of elders, who go to the nations of the earth to preach the gospel of Christ. After spending two or three years as missionaries, if they have converted a dozen souls and brought them into the Church, they think they have done a good work, which they certainly have. But here, the elders who are presiding over and teaching in these institutions in Zion, filled with the children of the Latter-day Saints, have an army of immortal souls before them to guide and teach, and to direct their minds, that they may be qualified to step forth and take hold of the Church and kingdom of God and build it up and bear it off triumphantly, after their fathers and elders are laid in the tomb. O what a mission is given to the sons of Ephraim, the elders of Israel, the Latter-day Saints! To warn the whole world of the judgments which are to come, preach the gospel to all people, gather the Saints from all nations, build up Zion, and prepare for the coming of the Son of Man, standing in holy places, while judgments waste the wicked.[67]

Like a well-disciplined army, each soldier must learn to do his duty without excessive worry about position or rank. Without faithful, lowly privates, generals would have no one to lead and the war would not be won.

What of the Gentiles? Are we not interested in gathering them into the fold? The obvious answer is "Yes, if they humble themselves and obey the gospel." Brigham Young, speaking again on the role Ephraim plays in the gathering of scattered Israel said,

Will we go to the Gentile nations to preach the Gospel? Yes, and gather out the Israelites, wherever they are mixed among the nations of the earth. What part or portion of them? The same part or portion that redeemed the house of Jacob, and saved them from perishing with famine in Egypt. When Jacob blessed the two sons of Joseph, "guiding his hands wittingly," he placed his right hand upon Ephraim, "and he blessed Joseph, and said, God, before whom my fathers

---

[67] Wilford Woodruff, <u>The Discourses of Wilford Woodruff</u>, p.104

Abraham and Isaac did walk, the God which fed me all my life long unto this day, the Angel which redeemed me from all evil, bless the lads," etc. Joseph was about to remove the old man's hands, and bringing his right hand upon the head of the oldest boy, saying— "Not so, my father; for this is the first born; put thy right hand upon his head. And his father refused, and said, I know it, my son, I know it: he also shall become a people, and he also shall be great; but truly his younger brother shall be greater than he, and his seed shall become a multitude of nations." Ephraim has become mixed with all the nations of the earth, and it is Ephraim that is gathering together.***It is Ephraim that I have been searching for all the days of my preaching, and that is the blood which ran in my veins when I embraced the Gospel. If there are any of the other tribes of Israel mixed with the Gentiles we are also searching for them. Though the Gentiles are cut off, do not suppose that we are not going to preach the Gospel among the Gentile nations, for they are mingled with the house of Israel, and when we send to the nations we do not seek for the Gentiles, because they are disobedient and rebellious. We want the blood of Jacob, and that of his father Isaac and Abraham, which runs in the veins of the people. There is a particle of it here, and another there, blessing the nations as predicted.***Take a family of ten children, for instance, and you may find nine of them purely of the Gentile stock, and one son or one daughter in that family who is purely of the Blood of Ephraim. It was in the veins of the father or mother, and was reproduced in the son or daughter, while all the rest of the family are Gentiles. You may think that is singular, but it is true. It is the house of Israel we are after, and we care not whether they come from the east, the west, the north, or the south; from China, Russia, England, California, North or South America, or some other locality; and it is the very lad on whom father Jacob laid his hands, that will save the house of Israel. The Book of Mormon came to Ephraim, for Joseph Smith was a pure Ephraimite, and The Book of Mormon was revealed to him, and while he lived he made it his business to search for those who believed the Gospel.[68]

From pre-mortal times, covenants were made and blessings earned. The great work of the gospel during this last dispensation is to find those with whom those covenants were made and help them renew them on earth that they might enjoy them eternally in the heavens. Alvin R. Dyer wrote,

---

[68] Journal of Discourses, Vol.2, p.268-269, Brigham Young, April 8, 1855

It is the good and honest of heart among the people of the world who most readily respond to the message of the Restoration as declared by the missionaries who bring it to them.[69]

What a glorious opportunity for those in whose veins flow the blood of chosen Ephraim! What a sobering responsibility to take the gospel to the nations. Elder Orson F. Whitney said,

> In preaching the gospel, to the world and gathering Israel from the nations, the Latter-day Saints—children of Ephraim—are helping to fulfil the covenant made by Jehovah with Abraham, Isaac and Jacob.[70]

To help the Father fulfil the covenants made with the ancient fathers is at once inspiring and challenging. The Prophet Joseph Smith urged his co-workers on by saying,

> Brethren, shall we not go on in so great a cause? Go forward and not backward. Courage, brethren; and on, on to the victory! Let your hearts rejoice, and be exceedingly glad. Let the earth break forth into singing. Let the dead speak forth anthems of eternal praise to the King Immanuel, who hath ordained, before the world was, that which would enable us to redeem them out of their prison; for the prisoners shall go free. (D&C 128:22)

Whether prisoners in the spirit world because liberating ordinances have not yet been performed, or prisoners here on the earth because of erroneous ideas or shackling habits, or bad behavior born of the philosophies of men, the gospel holds the liberating key. Are we just another people among the nameless billions who live out their mortal existence with little or no direction? Certainly not! With that divinely given charge and destiny, it would only be reasonable to expect some opposition.

---

[69] Alvin R. Dyer, Improvement Era, December 1970, p.125

[70] Orson F. Whitney, Conference Report, April 1928, p.58

CHAPTER 10

Ephraim and Temple Work

One would think that with the super-human responsibility of taking the gospel to every living creature on earth, that the overwhelming task of providing saving and exalting ordinances for the dead would be given to another group of people. Not so. Rulon S. Wells spoke in conference of our expanded responsibility,

> And now comes the great responsibility that rests upon that chosen few... Those who have died without a knowledge of the Gospel may, if they are honest in heart, be converted and brought to repentance when the Gospel is preached to them in the spirit world, but even as the question arose in the mind of Nicodemus with reference to the living, "How can a man be born when he is old," the question now might naturally arise: how can a man be born when he is dead ?[71]

To the Latter-day Saints the answer to Nicodemus' question is simple, we must build temples and enter into them, performing every ordinance on behalf of the dead that is necessary for them to enter into their future exaltation in eternity. President Joseph Fielding Smith informed us that only mortals can perform saving ordinances. Immortal beings (either disembodied spirits or resurrected beings) must wait upon us.

> Only mortals can perform temple ordinances. Will resurrected beings during the millennium actually take part in the endowment work of the temple along with mortal beings?

> The answer to this question is no! That is, they will not assist in performing the ordinances. Resurrected beings will assist in furnishing

---

[71] Rulon S. Wells, <u>Conference Report</u>, April 1932, p.70

information which is not otherwise available, but mortals will have to do the ordinance work in the temples.

Baptism, confirmation, ordination, endowment, and sealings all pertain to this mortal life and are ordinances required of those who are in mortality. Provision has been made for these ordinances to be performed vicariously for those who are worthy but who died without the opportunity in this life of receiving these ordinances in person.

You can readily see that it would be inconsistent for a resurrected being to come and be baptized for the dead. The resurrected person has passed to another sphere where the laws and blessings do not pertain to this mortal life. This is equally true of every other ordinance. If it were permissible for resurrected persons to come and do work in the temples, then there would be no reason for us in this mortal life to act vicariously for them, for they would do it for themselves.[72]

Erastus Snow further emphasized the importance of fulfilling the redemptive work for the dead. When one considers the countless billions who have already died, compared to the five and a half billion now alive on the earth, the comparison makes perfect sense.

Now the work of carrying the Gospel to the nations and gathering the people, mighty as it is, is not the chief, it is but laying the foundation for the still greater work of the redemption of the myriads of the dead of the seed of Israel that have perished without the fullness of the Gospel, who too are heirs to the promised blessings; but the time had not come when they passed away for the fulfillment of all that God had promised Abraham, Isaac and Jacob concerning their seed.[73]

It seems as though the work of the faithful sons of Ephraim will not be excused from their work associated with redeeming the dead even when they die. Erastus Snow said further,

All the Elders of this dispensation who prove faithful and magnify their calling in the flesh will, when they pass hence, continue their labors in the spirit world, retaining the same holy character and high responsibility that they assume here. And these men will be engaged

---

[72] Joseph Fielding Smith Jr., <u>Doctrines of Salvation</u>, Vol.2, p.178
[73] <u>Journal of Discourses</u>, Vol.23, p.186, Erastus Snow, May 6, 1882

there hunting up the remnants of their fathers of the house of Joseph through Ephraim and Manasseh.[74]

Even though Ephraim is being spread thin in order to accomplish all the Lord expects of us, we are still required to fulfill our foreordained missions. Joseph Fielding Smith taught us that,

It is Ephraim, today, who holds the priesthood. It is with Ephraim that the Lord has made covenant and has revealed the fulness of the everlasting gospel. It is Ephraim who is building temples and performing the ordinances in them for both the living and for the dead.[75]

What would be the reunion on the other side of the veil if we become distracted, disheartened, or through negligence, fail to perform our duty? Rulon S. Wells considered that possibility in one of his conference addresses,

It would indeed be a calamity if we should fail to do the part assigned to us in the accomplishment of the divine purpose as children of Abraham and descendants of Joseph and Ephraim, namely, performing the work for and in behalf of our ancestors who died without a knowledge of the Gospel, the work which they are no longer able to do for themselves, namely, baptisms and other ordinances in order that they too may become the sons and daughters of God, both in spirit and in body.[76]

Ephraim and the Building of the New Jerusalem

Although temple building is going on today at an unprecedented pace, there are yet more temples to be built. As Ephraim continues his tireless work, a great temple will eventually be built in a Divinely designated spot in Jackson County, Missouri. Brigham Young contemplated what would be necessary to build the New Jerusalem wherein the great temple would be constructed. He said,

Take the people in the east, west, north, and south who have obeyed the gospel, and, so far as the spiritual gifts are concerned, they are all of one heart and one mind, but not one soul knows how to build

---

[74] Journal of Discourses, Vol.23, p.187, Erastus Snow, May 6, 1882

[75] Joseph Fielding Smith Jr., Doctrines of Salvation, Vol.3, p.252 - p.253

[76] Rulon S. Wells, Conference Report, April 1932, p.71

up Zion. Not a man in all the realms and kingdoms that exist knows how to commence the foundation of the Zion of God in the latter days without revelation. If the people in the world could sanctify themselves and prepare themselves to build up Zion they might remain scattered, but they cannot, they must be gathered together to be taught, that they may sanctify themselves before the Lord and become of one heart and of one mind. By and by the Jews will be gathered to the land of their fathers, and the ten tribes, who wandered into the north, will be gathered home, and the blood of Ephraim, the second son of Joseph, who was sold into Egypt, which is to be found in every kingdom and nation under heaven, will be gathered from among the Gentiles, and the Gentiles who will receive and adhere to the principles of the gospel will be adopted and initiated into the family of Father Abraham, and Jesus will reign over His own and Satan will reign over his own. This will be the result.[77]

Some have misunderstood certain passages in The Book of Mormon about the building of the New Jerusalem. They seem to feel that the Lamanites will take charge of the building and the mighty sons of Ephraim will play a supportive role. President Joseph Fielding Smith clarifies the doctrine by saying,

Now do the scriptures teach that Ephraim, after doing all of this is to abdicate, or relinquish his place, and give it to the Lamanites and then receive orders from this branch of the "remnant of Jacob" in the building of the New Jerusalem? This certainly is inconsistent with the whole plan and with all that the Lord has revealed in the Doctrine and Covenants in relation to the establishment of Zion and the building of the New Jerusalem....

That the remnants of Joseph, found among the descendants of Lehi, will have part in this great work is certainly consistent, and the great work of this restoration, the building of the temple and the City of Zion, or New Jerusalem, will fall to the lot of the descendants of Joseph, but it is Ephraim who will stand at the head and direct the work.[78]

When will we return to Jackson County, Missouri and build up the New Jerusalem? The exact date has not been revealed to the rank and

---

[77] Journal of Discourses, Vol.12, p.38, Brigham Young, April 14th, 1867
[78] Joseph Fielding Smith Jr., Doctrines of Salvation, Vol.2, p.251

file of the Church. We can be comforted to know that we are where we are supposed to be for the present time. Melvin J. Ballard said,

> He has brought them to the right place. Joseph's blessings were to obtain above the blessings of his progenitors, even to the utmost bounds of the everlasting hills. It is no chance circumstance that we are here. Notwithstanding all the drivings, the sorrows and distresses, at Nauvoo and Missouri, the difficulties in gathering the Saints from the Old World—these were but God's providences in gathering his people to the right place.[79]

When we do return, it will be by the invitation of the living Prophet. The Lord described that return to "redeem Zion" in these words,

> Behold, I say unto you, the redemption of Zion must needs come by power;
>
> Therefore, I will raise up unto my people a man, who shall lead them like as Moses led the children of Israel.
>
> For ye are the children of Israel, and of the seed of Abraham, and ye must needs be led out of bondage by power, and with a stretched-out arm.
>
> And as your fathers were led at the first, even so shall the redemption of Zion be.
>
> Therefore, let not your hearts faint, for I say not unto you as I said unto your fathers: Mine angel shall go up before you, but not my presence.
>
> But I say unto you: Mine angels shall go up before you, and also my presence, and in time ye shall possess the goodly land. (D&C 103:15-20)

It is not to be thought that the entire Church will abandon their stronghold in the Rocky Mountains and return to Missouri. Wilford Woodruff recounts a meeting where the Prophet Joseph Smith was quizzing the brethren about their vision of the future of the church and kingdom. He said,

---

[79] Melvin J. Ballard, <u>Conference Report</u>, October 1924, p.29

On Sunday night the Prophet called on all who held the Priesthood to gather into the little log school house they had there. It was a small house, perhaps 14 feet square. But it held the whole of the Priesthood of The Church of Jesus Christ of Latter-day Saints who were then in the town of Kirtland, and who had gathered together to go off in Zion's camp. That was the first time I ever saw Oliver Cowdery, or heard him speak; the first time I ever saw Brigham Young and Heber C. Kimball, and the two Pratts, and Orson Hyde and many others. There were no Apostles in the Church then except Joseph Smith and Oliver Cowdery. When we got together the Prophet called upon the Elders of Israel with him to bear testimony of this work. Those that I have named spoke and a good many that I have not named, bore their testimonies. When they got through the Prophet said, "Brethren, I have been very much edified and instructed in your testimonies here tonight, but I want to say to you before the Lord, that you know no more concerning the destinies of this Church and kingdom than a babe upon its mother's lap. You don't comprehend it." I was rather surprised. He said, "It is only a little handful of Priesthood you see here tonight, but this Church will fill North and South America—it will fill the world." Among other things he said, "It will fill the Rocky Mountains. There will be tens of thousands of Latter-day Saints who will be gathered in the Rocky Mountains, and there they will open the door for the establishing of the Gospel among the Lamanites, who will receive the Gospel and their endowments and the blessings of God. This people will go into the Rocky Mountains; they will there build temples to the Most High. They will raise up a posterity there, and the Latter-day Saints who dwell in these mountains will stand in the flesh until the coming of the Son of Man. The Son of Man will come to them while in the Rocky Mountains."

I name these things because I want to bear testimony before God, angels and men that mine eyes behold the day, and have beheld for the last fifty years of my life, the fulfillment of that prophecy. [80]

As future prophesied events are contemplated, the mind begins to reel. What would it be like to have the privilege of helping construct the New Jerusalem? Even further, we may be there to welcome the "Lost 10 Tribes" as they return from their nearly three millennia of exile. Not

---

[80] Wilford Woodruff, <u>Conference Report</u>, April 1898, p. 57

having been privileged to have the fulness of the temple blessings, the sons and daughters of Ephraim will again enjoy a signal opportunity. President Wilford Woodruff described their return and the part Ephraim will play after they return.

> Again, here are the ten tribes of Israel; we know nothing about them only what the Lord has said by his prophets. There are prophets among them, and by and by they will come along, and they will smite the rocks, and the mountains of ice will flow down at their presence, and a highway will be cast up before them, and they will come to Zion, receive their endowments, and be crowned under the hands of the children of Ephraim, and there are persons before me in this assembly today who will assist to give them their endowments. They will receive their blessings and endowments, from under the children of Ephraim, who are the first fruits of the kingdom of God in their dispensation, and the men will have to be ordained and receive their priesthood and endowments in the land of Zion, according to the revelations of God.[81]

Rich Blessings on the Head of Ephraim

President Woodruff further explained that the 10 Lost Tribes had long since fallen into a state of unbelief and needed the restorative effects of the fulness of the Gospel. That redemptive process was to come through Ephraim.

> But they, like the Jews, have fallen through the same example of unbelief, and now, in the last days, the kingdom of God has to be taken from the Gentiles, and restored back to every branch and tribe of the house of Israel; and when it is restored to them, it must go back with all its gifts, and blessings, and priesthood which it possessed when it was taken from them. But the Lord has said that in restoring these blessings to the children of Abraham, that he would be inquired of by the house of Israel, to do it for them. But from what branch or part of the house of Israel will the Lord look for this petition or request to issue, if not from the Latter-day Saints? For we are out of the tribe of Joseph through the loins of Ephraim, who has been as a mixed cake among the Gentiles, and are the first fruits of

---

[81] The Discourses of Wilford Woodruff, p.119. Journal of Discourses 4:231-232, February 22, 1857

the kingdom, and the Lord has given unto us the kingdom and priest-hood and keys thereof. Hence the Lord will require us to ask for those blessings which are promised unto Israel, and to labor for their salvation.[82]

There is no doubt from what has been written about the children of Ephraim that we are in line to receive the "richer blessings" of all that God has prepared for His children. President Joseph Fielding Smith, in addressing this topic, also reminds us that all the other tribes will receive their blessings through our services.

Temple work—I take it we, the members of the Church, most of us of the tribe of Ephraim, are of the remnant of Jacob. We know it to be the fact that the Lord called upon the descendants of Ephraim to commence his work in the earth in these last days. We know further that he has said that he set Ephraim, according to the promises of his birthright, at the head, Ephraim receives the "richer blessings," these blessings being those of presidency or direction. The keys are with Ephraim. It is Ephraim who is to be endowed with power to bless and give to the other tribes, including the Lamanites, their blessings. All the other tribes of Jacob, including the Lamanites, are to be crowned with glory in Zion by the hands of Ephraim.[83]

One wonders if it is the lax attitude of the parents or the lack-adaisical approach of the youth of Zion which would cause them not to take advantage of the great saving and exalting blessings of the temple. How could they then participate in administering those blessings to the other tribes of Israel, if they have not availed themselves of those blessings? Hyrum G. Smith voiced the displeasure of the Lord with the youth of his day for not preparing and going to the temple. Unfortu-nately, we have not improved much since that time. He said,

The blessings of the Lord are with this people, yet in spite of this condition there are a few things existing in our midst with which the Lord is not pleased. I have noticed this particularly among some of our young people. Our young people are choice, they are the sons and daughters of Israel, the chosen blood of Ephraim, upon whom

---

[82] The Discourses of Wilford Woodruff, p.117 - p.118, Journal of Discourses 4:232-233, February 22, 1857

[83] Joseph Fielding Smith Jr., Doctrines of Salvation, Vol.2, p.250 - p.251

responsibility rests in this age. The thing to which I specially refer that is not pleasing in the sight of the Lord, nor to our faithful fathers and mothers in Israel, is the fact that too many of our boys and girls, choice young men and women, are not availing themselves of the blessings of the Lord as administered in the Holy Temples. To the Latter-day Saints, the Lord has given His law, which provides that if they abide not by it, there will come a time when there will be weeping and wailing, distress and sorrow, and we do not have to wait until after death, either, because we see these conditions in this life, because of our disobedience, and because of the fact that altogether too many of our young people, when they marry, accept the laws of the land only, and not the laws of God, both of which are legal and lawful as far as this life is concerned, but only the laws of God are valid after death. This conduct on the part of many of our young people, to marry outside the Temples, or to marry those not of their own faith is not pleasing in the sight of the Lord.[84]

Although our knowledge about the Lost 10 Tribes is fragmentary at best, we are assured that they have not been forgotten by the Lord. They are intact as a group, are being prepared by their prophets for their magnificent return, and will come to Ephraim for their blessings. President Joseph Fielding Smith summarizes our current understanding,

The Ten Tribes Led Away—The Ten Tribes were taken by force out of the land the Lord gave to them. Many of them mixed with the peoples among whom they were scattered. A large portion, however, departed in one body into the north and disappeared from the rest of the world. Where they went and where they are, we do not know. That they are intact we must believe, else how shall the scriptures be fulfilled? There are too many prophecies concerning them and their return in a body, for us to ignore this fact. Elder Orson F. Whitney, writing of this said: "It is maintained by some that the lost tribes of Israel—those carried into captivity about 725 B.C.—are no longer a distinct people; that they exist only in a scattered condition, mixed with the nations among which they were taken by their captors, the conquering Assyrians. If this be true, and those tribes were not intact at the time Joseph and Oliver received the keys of the gathering, why did they make so pointed a reference to "the leading of the ten tribes from the land of the north?" This, too, after a

---

84 Hyrum G. Smith, <u>Conference Report</u>, April 1916, p.61

general allusion to "the gathering of Israel from the four parts of the earth." What need to particularize as to the Ten Tribes, if they were no longer a distinct people? And why do our Articles of Faith give those tribes a special mention?" — Saturday Night Thoughts, p. 174.[85]

There are those in the Church who suggest that Judah will receive their promised blessings from prophets raised up unto themselves. The logic is that the Jews are so set in their ways that the only ones they would accept as their leaders would be those from among them. President Joseph Fielding Smith suggests a different approach.

Judah also is to be gathered, but to Jerusalem and Palestine. The tribes of Israel will come to Zion where they will be crowned and eventually many of them will find their way back to the land of their inheritance, for so it has been promised. (See Ether 13:10-11.) When Judah is gathered, and we may be happy in the knowledge that he is being gathered, he too must receive his blessings from his brother Ephraim.[86]

Those keys, vouchsafed to Joseph Smith and Oliver Cowdery in the Kirtland Temple in April 1836, make possible the greatest blessings the Father has in store for His children. Without the sealing power, the whole earth would be utterly wasted at the coming of the Savior (D&C 2:1-3). Not surprising, Ephraim plays a major role in administering those exalting blessings to the remainder of our Father's children. How privileged we are to participate in these and future events! It is cause for serious consideration when we contemplate our role in these great events.

The "Crowning Blessings" From Ephraim—It is Ephraim, today, who holds the Priesthood. It is with Ephraim that the Lord has made covenant and has revealed the fulness of the everlasting Gospel. It is Ephraim who is building temples and performing the ordinances in them for both the living and the dead. When the "lost tribes" come — and it will be a most wonderful sight and a marvelous thing when they do come to Zion — in fulfillment of the promises made through Isaiah and Jeremiah, they will have to receive the crowning blessings from their brother Ephraim, the "first-born" in Israel.[87]

---

[85] Joseph Fielding Smith Jr., The Way to Perfection, p.130-131

[86] Joseph Fielding Smith Jr., The Way to Perfection, p.126

[87] Joseph Fielding Smith Jr., The Way to Perfection, p.125

Could the vision of those things yet future, encourage all of us to enter the temples ourselves and teach our children to go there to receive their endowments, in preparation of participating in giving those same blessings to the other tribes of Israel? We can and must do better in our quest for understanding of our Father's plan for the redemption of all His children.

CHAPTER 11

Ephraim and the Perfecting of the Saints

As the storm clouds darken around us, as "evil men and seducers shall wax worse and worse, deceiving, and being deceived" (2 Timothy 3:13), and as the righteous look anxiously towards the heavens for the return of the Son of Man, it is imperative that we respond to the Savior's question to the Nephites: "What manner of men ought ye to be" (3 Nephi 27:27)? He also, in that same verse, gave us the answer: "Verily I say unto you, even as I am." The perfecting process of the Saints must go on. The Prophet Joseph Smith said,

> When you climb up a ladder, you must begin at the bottom, and ascend step by step, until you arrive at the top; and so it is with the principles of the Gospel — you must begin with the first, and go on until you learn all the principles of exaltation. But it will be a great while after you have passed through the veil before you will have learned them. It is not all to be comprehended in this world; it will be a great work to learn our salvation and exaltation even beyond the grave.[88]

However, we are not exempted from doing all we can do in moving ourselves and our fellow human beings along the pathway to perfection. Melvin J. Ballard said,

> How we ought to rejoice in knowing that they are found and that we are the children of Joseph. These are the chosen people of God, and yet not in boastfulness, but as the natural inheritors of blessings and privileges. We should arise to the Lord's expectations; and through

---

[88] <u>Teachings of the Prophet Joseph Smith</u>, Section Six 1843-44 p.348

his providing we ought to become distinguished and unlike the world, a peculiar people... With such possibilities, nothing overlooked on the part of the Lord, why shall we not arise and shine, that our light indeed may be a standard to the nations that we may become the salt of the earth? The power is in this Church, to become a mighty people.[89]

One cannot embrace the fulness of the gospel of Jesus Christ without it having a profound effect on every aspect of his life. Not only is the person who joins the Church perfected by application of gospel principles, but all people with whom he associates must also be perfected.

There is one responsibility which no man can evade; that responsibility is his personal influence. Man's unconscious influence is the silent, subtle radiation of personality—the effect of his words and his actions on others. This radiation is tremendous. Every moment of life man is changing, to a degree, the life of the whole world.

Every man has an atmosphere which is affecting every other man. He cannot escape for one moment from this radiation of his character, this constant weakening or strengthening of others. Man cannot evade the responsibility by merely saying it is an unconscious influence.

Man can select the qualities he would permit to be radiated. he can cultivate sweetness, calmness, trust, generosity, truth, justice, loyalty, nobility, and make them vitally active in his character. And by these qualities he will constantly affect the world.

This radiation, to which I refer, comes from what a person really is, not from what he pretends to be. Every man by his mere living is radiating either sympathy, sorrow, morbidness, cynicism, or happiness and hope or any one of a hundred other qualities.

Life is a state of radiation and absorption. To exist is to radiate; to exist is to be the recipient of radiation.[90]

President Joseph Fielding Smith emphasized the far-reaching, positive effects the gospel has had on our ancestors when they joined the Church and emigrated to the valleys of the mountains. He said,

---

[89] Melvin J. Ballard, <u>Conference Report</u>, October 1927, p.70
[90] David O. McKay (Given at BYU, April 27, 1948)

And so the gospel has benefited them temporally as well as spiritually, and we all know that it has benefited them morally, that we are better by far in every particular than we could have been had we remained, or our parents remained, and we had been born to them in the countries from whence they came. The Church today numbers many many thousands and they are of the house of Israel, principally of the tribe of Ephraim—Ephraim having received the birthright in Israel and the mission to stand at the head, to perform a work for his fellow kinsmen of the other tribes in the dispensation of the fulness of times in which we live.[91]

Ridding Ourselves of the Gentile Nature

Perhaps the vision of how perfected we can become has not yet been achieved. Combining quotes from several of his sermons, President Brigham Young said on the topic,

> Ephraim has become mixed with all the nations of the earth, and it is Ephraim that is gathering together. ***We are gathering the people as fast as we can. We are gathering them to make Saints of them and of ourselves. ***We have been gathered to the valleys of these mountains for the express purpose of purifying ourselves, that we may become polished stones in the temple of God. We are here for the purpose of establishing the Kingdom of God on the earth. To be prepared for this work it has been necessary to gather us out from the nations and countries of the world, for if we had remained in those lands we could not have received the ordinances of the holy Priesthood of the Son of God, which are necessary for the perfection of the Saints preparatory to his coming.[92]

In many respects the Church has become an "Ensign to the Nations" (Isaiah 5:26 and 2 Nephi 15:26). It is difficult (perhaps inappropriate) to point to the perfecting influence of the gospel on the lives of members of the Church, without giving the impression that we are better than others. However, we cannot escape the fact that the gospel was restored for the perfecting of the saints (Ephesians 4:11-14). There have been and will always be, until the Second Coming of the Savior, detractors who accuse us of being usurpers, imitators of the true gospel. Melvin J. Ballard said,

---

[91] Joseph Fielding Smith Jr., <u>Doctrines of Salvation</u>, Vol.3, p.256 - p.257

[92] <u>Discourses of Brigham Young</u>, p.121

God bless us that we shall treasure our heritage, that we shall recognize that we are to do an unusual thing. We are not called to be imitators, we are called to be exemplars to the world, a light that shall shine until the day will come when from the east to the west, the north to the south, they will come, not to look upon our lands nor our fields nor our factories, but to learn of our ways that they may walk in our paths, and thereby find peace, preservation and salvation now and eternally.[93]

A Safe Environment to be Perfected

The emigrating of the Saints to the valleys of the mountains, as with every other aspect dealing with the winding up scene, was no mistake. Elder LeGrand Richards spoke about the prophesied gathering of scattered Israel with flourishing Ephraim at the forefront. It appears to have been necessary for Ephraim to gather in the isolated tops of the mountains to provide a safe environment where the Saints could be perfected in preparation for their assuming their rightful position as an ensign or example of godliness to the nations. Elder Richards also talked about the Church becoming an ensign to the nations and the envy of Ephraim and Judah departing.

> "The envy also of Ephraim shall depart, and the adversaries of Judah shall be cut off: Ephraim shall not envy Judah, and Judah shall not vex Ephraim" (Isa. 11:13). We are from Ephraim. The Lord expects us, since we are the custodians of his gospel as restored in these latter days, according to my understanding, to extend the hand of friendship to Judah, because after all we are all descendants of the prophets Abraham, Isaac, and Jacob, and we come under the promises that through their descendants should all the nations of the earth be blessed.***I do not know how the enmity and the envy between Ephraim and Judah can disappear except that we of the house of Ephraim, who have the custody of the gospel, should lead out in trying to bring to this branch of the house of Israel the blessings of the restored gospel...
>
> Now we have lived to see the first part of that prediction literally fulfilled. He has gathered Israel into these valleys of the mountains according to his promise. He has set up an ensign unto the nations.

---

[93] Melvin J. Ballard, <u>Conference Report</u>, October 1927, p.70

It seems to me that no thoughtful, honest person could examine what the Lord has done in the establishment of this Church, his kingdom on the earth, and then give any mortal man or group of men the credit for what has been accomplished. It has been the God of heaven that has done this, according to the words of the prophets.[94]

Is it easier for those of Ephraim to accept the gospel truths and live them than for the rest of our Father's children? Charles W. Penrose suggested that this might be the case because of our pre-mortal diligence.

Truth, speaking of it in the abstract, has no beginning. Truth is eternal, without beginning of days or end of life. The power and ability to receive truth is a great thing—that is a gift which I believe is largely bestowed upon the Latter-day Saints. I believe there is something in our racial connection which has to do with this...Now, I think that we who are of that race, are naturally so disposed; that there is something with us that tends to our willingness to accept the truth when it comes from God. I do not mean to say that this is confined to us, but that particularly those who are of the house of Ephraim are ready to receive the word and act according to it as the Lord shall direct.[95]

Elder Neal A. Maxwell cautioned the youth of today against assuming an attitude of superiority based on their chosen position during these last days. He said,

Tonight I would like to talk principally to the young men of the Aaronic Priesthood about the responsibility you have to live in such a way that you can be a good influence in your homes, whatever the conditions there may be, and so that you can qualify to do all the Lord expects of you during your lifetime.

Young men, I do not believe that you are here upon the earth at this time by accident. I believe you qualified in the premortal life to come into mortality at a time when great things would be required of you. I believe you demonstrated before you came here that you were capable of being trusted under unusually difficult circumstances—that you could measure up to the most difficult challenges.

---

[94] LeGrand Richards, <u>Conference Report</u>, October 1956, p.23
[95] Charles W. Penrose, <u>Conference Report</u>, October 1922, p.21-22

Don't misunderstand me. I don't suggest that you are inherently better than or superior to any of the other generations that have come to the earth. You do not automatically qualify for any more blessings or advantages than anyone else who has lived since the earth was created. You can go astray, become involved in transgression, and incur the judgments of God as readily as any who have preceded you here. In fact, you live in an environment in which it is probably as easy to disqualify yourselves in this way as any generation has ever experienced. But God trusts that you will not. He relies upon you to keep yourselves eligible to accomplish the monumental tasks that he expects you to achieve.

My beloved friends, you are the vanguard of the righteous spirits to be infused into the Church in the last days. Back beyond time, it was so determined, and you were prepared—before the foundations of the world—to help save others in the latter-day world.

You cannot keep that resplendent rendezvous if you become like the world! Make your righteous marks on the world instead of being spotted by the world.

Be true, now, to your emotions of long ago when, as the Lord set in motion His plan of Salvation and laid the foundation of this earth, "The morning stars sang together, and all the sons (and daughters) of God shouted for joy" (Job 38:7).[96]

As ever, the Destroyer is attempting to minimize the damaging effects to his kingdom that the Saints can make. Among his most effective tools are discord and divisiveness. Joseph F. Smith cautioned the Saints,

A striking peculiarity of the Saints gathered from all parts of the earth is that they are almost universally of the blood of Ephraim. If they have received the Holy Ghost they are of one spirit, so that whatever creates a discord in the spirit and unity of the Saints is of evil origin. The Spirit of God never begets strife, nor does it set up and insist on distinctions among those who have been its recipients.[97]

---

[96] Elder Neal A. Maxwell, Young Adult Fireside on Temple Square, 23 June 1985
[97] Joseph Fielding Smith, Gospel Doctrine, p.115

Preserved to Come Forth At This Time

In the not-too distant future, a meeting of unparalleled magnitude will be held at Adam-ondi-Ahman (D&C 116; Daniel 7:9-14). As many as one hundred million people will be there, representing the righteous from the very beginning of time until our day (Daniel 7:9-14). Because of the prominence of Ephraim in the preparations of the earth for the Second Coming of Christ, it stands to reason that many of the valiant leaders and members now living will be invited to attend those meetings. In fact, of the four groups who will be represented (i.e. Resurrected beings, translated beings, disembodied spirits, and mortals), Ephraim will likely comprise the majority of the last category. He who has borne the weight of the burden of preparing the world during the heat of the day, will be honored among his brethren. President Joseph Fielding Smith promised, "Zion shall be the gathering place of Ephraim and his fellows, upon whose heads shall be conferred 'the richer blessings.'"[98]

If we are going to qualify for the blessing of being invited to Adam-ondi-Ahman, as well as the other great events yet future, we are going to have to step up and assume our rightful role as leaders in this latter-day kingdom. Bishop H. Burke Peterson addressing the youth said,

> My dear friends, you are a royal generation. You were preserved to come to the earth in this time for a special purpose. Not just a few of you, but all of you. There are things for each of you to do that no one else can do as well as you. If you do not prepare to do them, they will not be done. Your mission is unique and distinctive for you. Please don't make another have to take your place. He or she can't do it as well as you can. If you will let Him, I testify that our Father in Heaven will walk with you through the journey of life and inspire you to know your special purpose here.[99]

It takes a hearty soul to fulfill all that God has laid upon the shoulders of His saints in these latter days. Although parents may complain, at times, because of the adventuresome spirit of their children and their stubbornness when they make up their minds, yet those very qualities are among the lengthy list of attributes necessary to withstand the trials of the latter days. Brigham Young assured us that we are equal to the challenge.

---

[98] Joseph Fielding Smith Jr., <u>Doctrines of Salvation</u>, Vol.3, p.69 - p.70
[99] H. Burke Peterson, "Your Life Has a Purpose," <u>New Era</u>, May 1979, p. 5

No hardship will discourage these men [descendants of Ephraim]; they will penetrate the deepest wilds and overcome almost insurmountable difficulties to develop the treasures of the earth, to further their indomitable spirit of adventure.[100]

Chosen Ephraim

How can we be so sure that it is us the prophets have spoken of for so many years? Isn't it presumptuous to claim the rights of chosen Ephraim as our own? The world would certainly have you believe it is. However, by revelation, the Lord calls patriarchs (D&C 107:39) in His restored Church. For years those patriarchs have been giving blessings in the church to countless thousands of men and women, boys and girls. There has been an almost total declaration that the person is either from Ephraim or Manasseh. President Joseph Fielding Smith said,

> If the patriarch who is here should lay his hands upon your head and declare your genealogy, he would tell you...that, almost without exception, you are the descendants of Ephraim.[101]

Even though those descending through Manasseh are favored along with those from Ephraim, Hyrum G. Smith draws the following distinction,

> At the present time in the Church the great majority of those receiving their blessings are declared to be of the house and lineage of Ephraim, while many others are designated as members of the house of Manasseh; but up to the present time we have discovered that those who are leaders in Israel, no matter where they come from, no matter what nation they have come out of, are of Ephraim; while the blood of Manasseh is found in the tribes and nations of the Indians of North and South America. They are great, they are wonderfully blessed, but Ephraim seems to prevail in the greater blessings, greater in responsibility, and in faithfulness to the Lord's work. And so people have wondered about it. Why do the patriarchs declare that most of us are of Ephraim? It is my testimony that "today" is the day of Ephraim.[102]

---

[100] Brigham Young, <u>Discourses</u> p. 670
[101] Joseph Fielding Smith Jr., <u>Doctrines of Salvation</u>, Vol.3, p.248
[102] Hyrum G. Smith, <u>Conference Report</u>, April 1929, page 123

If one were to do a study of those who have been honored to sit in the highest councils of the Church, it would not be surprising to find that, almost without exception, they have been through the tribe of Ephraim. Joseph Fielding Smith again re-emphasized the reason.

There is the fact revealed through the Prophet Joseph Smith, who was of the lineage of Joseph through the loins of Ephraim, that the majority of the people who have been first to receive the gospel and priesthood of the latter-day dispensation, are descendants of some of the house of Ephraim scattered among the nations.[103]

There is an imperative need among Latter-day Saints to recognize the power and the privilege associated with our lineage. Patriarch Hyrum G. Smith said, "Now, my brethren and sisters, let me urge that we, both old and young, begin to appreciate our blessings."[104]

Apostle Melvin J. Ballard gave a very similar and stirring plea, not only that we recognize our destiny but also that we take advantage of the means God has placed in our hands to succeed,

May God bless us to keep our eye upon our glorious destiny and recognize that within our hands are the means of accomplishing such an end, and not be blind to our privileges.[105]

Why is the sense of urgency about perfecting the saints being echoed so strongly by leaders for over the past hundred and fifty years? What is the big hurry? Why is our dispensation any different than any that have gone before? The Prophet Joseph Smith gave the answer,

I would advise all the Saints to go with their might and gather together all their living relatives to this place, that they may be sealed and saved, that they may be prepared against the day that the destroying angel goes forth; and if the whole Church should go to with all their might to save their dead, seal their posterity, and gather their living friends, and spend none of their time in behalf of the world, they would hardly get through before night would come, when no man can work; and my only trouble at the present time is concerning ourselves, that the Saints will be divided, broken up, and

---

[103] Joseph Fielding Smith Jr., <u>Doctrines of Salvation</u>, Vol.3, p.247
[104] Hyrum G. Smith, <u>Conference Report</u>, October 1922, p.50
[105] Melvin J. Ballard, <u>Conference Report</u>, October 1927, p.70

scattered, before we get our salvation secure; for there are so many fools in the world for the devil to operate upon, it gives him the advantage oftentimes.[106]

That seems to be the summation of the entire matter. Some, as in pre-earth life, will not take full advantage of their foreordained privileges by failing to make the effort to move toward perfection here on earth. Others will forget their own selfish desires and work themselves into immortal glory. Rulon S. Wells talked about the natural selection process by which we, not God, determines whether we are chosen or whether our greatness will end with having been called.

> We live in a day when the children of Israel are again to be gathered after their long dispersion. We have heard something of the return of the Jews, the tribe of Judah, to the land of their inheritance, even Palestine; but we are not of that tribe but of the tribe of Joseph, "that bright and glorious morning star," and particularly through Ephraim, his son, and are now being gathered on this the land of Joseph, given to him and his seed as an everlasting inheritance—a land choice above all other lands, the land of liberty, even the land of America. We are of that lineage and are now being gathered, having given heed to the call of the Gospel, hearing the voice of the true shepherd, even as we did in our former estate when we were counted among the great and noble ones; but now as then, many are called but few are chosen. The natural selection still goes on.[107]

What a shame and a disappointment to have qualified through pre-mortal diligence to be numbered among the "noble and great ones" and then because of pre-occupation with things of this world, fail in our diligence to fulfill our destiny. It certainly is not because He has too many valiant sons and daughters that the Lord calls for our services. Isaiah formulated the simple question we must constantly ask: "Watchman, what of the night? Watchman, what of the night" (Isaiah 21:11)? Ephraim has undoubtedly been called and assigned to be the "watchman" during these final scenes incident to the Second Coming. It is relatively simple to live the gospel and avoid temptations when the sun is shining or the Savior is standing in our midst. But what of the night, when Satan reigns and desolations abound? What of the prophesied

---

[106] Teachings of the Prophet Joseph Smith, Section Six 1843-44 p.330
[107] Rulon S. Wells, Conference Report, April 1932, p.70

season when men seemed to have forgotten how to reason, as they run wildly around "Ever learning, and never able to come to the knowledge of the truth" (2 Timothy 3:7)?

The mind-chilling vision shown to Enoch by the pre-mortal Savior is being fulfilled today at an unprecedented rate. "And he beheld Satan; and he had a great chain in his hand, and it veiled the whole face of the earth with darkness; and he looked up and laughed, and his angels rejoiced" (Moses 7:26).

There is an increasing need for our dedicated, unwavering services. The storm clouds will continue to darken, the love of man will wax colder and colder, atrocities will become more disgusting among the wicked of the world. As the Spirit is withdrawn from the wicked, unspeakable horrors will abound. The Lord said of the time just before His prophesied coming,

But few shall stand to receive an inheritance.

I, the Lord, am angry with the wicked; I am holding my Spirit from the inhabitants of the earth.

I have sworn in my wrath, and decreed wars upon the face of the earth, and the wicked shall slay the wicked, and fear shall come upon every man;

And the Saints also shall hardly escape; nevertheless, I, the Lord, am with them, and will come down in heaven from the presence of my Father and consume the wicked with unquenchable fire.

And behold, this is not yet, but by and by.

Wherefore, seeing that I, the Lord, have decreed all these things upon the face of the earth, I will that my saints should be assembled upon the land of Zion;

And that every man should take righteousness in his hands and faithfulness upon his loins, and lift a warning voice unto the inhabitants of the earth; and declare both by word and by flight that desolation shall come upon the wicked (D&C 63:31-37).

All of the silver and gold, lands and possessions that we may accumulate, will be of little value if we are not prepared for the Second Coming of Christ. All the degrees, honors and accolades man can bestow upon us will be of little consequence if we have failed to move toward perfection ourselves and been dilatory in our responsibilities to prepare the world for the Second Coming. Wilford Woodruff seemed to have this same theme in mind as he reissued the challenge to the Latter-day Saints to become a Zion people,

> We are called of God. We have been gathered from the distant nations, and our lives have been hid with Christ in God, but we have not known it. The Lord has been watching over us from the hour of our birth. We are of the seed of Ephraim, and of Abraham, and of Joseph, who was sold into Egypt, and these are the instruments that God has kept in the spirit world to come forth in these latter days to take hold of this kingdom and build it up. These are my sentiments with regard to the Latter-day Saints. I will repeat what I have often said—there is no power beneath the heavens that can remove Zion out of her place, or destroy this Church and kingdom, as long as the people do the will of God, for he will sustain them, and overrule the acts of their enemies for their good and for the final triumph of his truth in the earth... We should not permit houses and land, gold and silver, nor any of this world's goods to draw us aside from pursuing the great object which God has sent us to perform. Our aim is high, our destiny is high, and we should never disappoint our Father, nor the heavenly hosts who are watching over us. We should not disappoint the millions in the spirit world, who too are watching over us with an interest and anxiety that have hardly entered into our hearts to conceive of. These are great and mighty things which God requires of us. We would not be worthy of salvation, we would not be worthy of eternal lives in the kingdom of our God, if anything could turn us away from the truth or from the love of it.[108]

Considering the summation of the entire matter of Ephraim, would we not do well to encourage each other with Joseph's stirring charge,

> Brethren, shall we not go on in so great a cause? Go forward and not backward. Courage, brethren; and on, on to the victory! Let your hearts rejoice, and be exceedingly glad. Let the earth break forth into singing. Let the dead speak forth anthems of eternal praise to the King Immanuel, who hath ordained, before the world was, that

---

[108] Journal of Discourses, Vol.22, p.234, Wilford Woodruff, June 26, 1881

which would enable us to redeem them out of their prison; for the prisoners shall go free.

Let the mountains shout for joy, and all ye valleys cry aloud; and all ye seas and dry lands tell the wonders of your Eternal King! And ye rivers, and brooks, and rills, flow down with gladness. Let the woods and all the trees of the field praise the Lord; and ye solid rocks weep for joy! And let the sun, moon, and the morning stars sing together, and let all the sons of God shout for joy! And let the eternal creations declare his name forever and ever! And again I say, how glorious is the voice we hear from heaven, proclaiming in our ears, glory, and salvation, and honor, and immortality, and eternal life; kingdoms, principalities, and powers!

Behold, the great day of the Lord is at hand; and who can abide the day of his coming, and who can stand when he appeareth? For he is like a refiner's fire, and like fuller's soap; and he shall sit as a refiner and purifier of silver, and he shall purify the sons of Levi, and purge them as gold and silver, that they may offer unto the Lord an offering in righteousness. Let us, therefore, as a church and a people, and as Latter-day Saints, offer unto the Lord an offering in righteousness; and let us present in his holy temple, when it is finished, a book containing the records of our dead, which shall be worthy of all acceptation (D&C 128:22-24)

Appendix 1

The Second Gathering of the Literal Seed

The Tenth Article of Faith of The Church of Jesus Christ of Latter-day Saints declares: "We believe in the literal gathering of Israel." There are twenty-six sections in the Doctrine and Covenants that confirm the thesis that the literal blood of Israel is in the majority of the Church membership today. Further support of this literal gathering is given in The Book of Mormon, the Pearl of Great Price, by presidents of the Church, and members of the Quorum of the Twelve.[109]

The Covenant of Abraham

Father Abraham was promised that "In [his] seed shall all the kindreds of the earth be blessed" (3 Nephi 20:27; Genesis 12:1-3). The Pearl of Great Price establishes that this blessing to Abraham would be fulfilled through "the literal seed, or the seed of the body" (Abraham 2:11).

In reiterating those who would again "drink of the fruit of the vine" with him on the earth at a future great meeting (D&C 27:5), the Lord named "Joseph and Jacob and Isaac, and Abraham, your fathers, by whom the promises remain" (D&C 27:10). The designation of these great patriarchs as "your fathers, by whom the promises remain" confirms that the early brethren were literal descendants and also that the covenants or promises made to them were still in effect and not yet fulfilled.

Following the Latter-day Saints being driven out of Missouri, in 1834 the Lord revealed to them that the redemption of Zion would come and that he would raise up a man to lead them as Moses led the children of

---

[109] The declaration of Latter-day Saints being the literal seed of Israel has been made by modern-day prophets and apostles periodically throughout the history of the Church. Most recent verifications may be seen in President Ezra Taft Benson's "A Witness and A Warning," Deseret Book, 1988; Elder Bruce R. McConkie, "A New Witness for the Articles of Faith," Deseret Book, 1985; and Elder Russell M. Nelson, BYU devotional address November 22, 1988.

Israel "For ye are the children of Israel, and of the seed of Abraham" (D&C 103:15-17). He further verified that they would be led as their "fathers" were led and he gave promise of angelic forerunners as he had to their "fathers" (vv. 18-19). Upon the completion of the Kirtland Temple two years later, the Lord appeared and accepted that temple, and Elias also appeared. Elias "committed the dispensation of the gospel of Abraham, saying that in us and our seed all generations after us should be blessed" (D&C 110:1-10, 12). Thus the keys or directing power for the fulfillment of the promise made to Abraham that through his literal seed all nations would be blessed was restored.

In an earlier revelation, the Lord had instructed the saints to "renounce war and proclaim peace, and seek diligently to turn the hearts of the children to their *fathers*, and the hearts of the *fathers* to the children" (D&C 98:16; italics added).

In section eighty-four, the Lord traced for latter-day Israel the Melchizedek Priesthood authority from Moses to Abraham and from Abraham to Adam (D&C 84:6-16). He then spoke of the responsibilities of this priesthood and the priesthood of Aaron and of their sons making "an acceptable offering and sacrifice in the house of the Lord" in the New Jerusalem (vv. 18-32). Although indirectly this shows that Moses' and Aaron's literal seed, who are also literal seed of Abraham, are to be involved in the latter-day New Jerusalem temple.

Joseph Smith Fulfills Abraham's Covenant

In March of 1838, the Prophet Joseph answered certain questions on the writings of Isaiah. His answers were all prefaced by "thus saith the Lord," showing that they were given to him by revelation. He identified the rod spoken of in Isaiah 11:1 as "a servant in the hands of Christ, who is partly a descendant of Jesse as well as of Ephraim, or of the house of Joseph, on whom is laid much power" (D&C 113:3-4). Jesse is the father of Kind David and of the lineage of Judah. The descendant of Jesse (Judah) and Joseph is undoubtedly Joseph Smith himself, although in his modesty the Prophet did not identify himself in that role. He was given power to translate The Book of Mormon (D&C 20:8) which would fulfill the last part of the prophecy. Joseph Smith further interpreted the root of Jesse spoken of in Isaiah 11:10 as "a descendant of Jesse, as well as of Joseph, unto whom rightly belongs the priesthood, and the keys of the kingdom, for an ensign, and for the gathering of my people in the last days" (D&C 113:5-6). That the priesthood rightly belonged to Joseph Smith is evidenced by the Angel Moroni's message to him in September of 1823 that "God had a work for [him] to do" (JS-H 1:33). He was foreordained to his very work in the premortal council (TPJS 365). The keys of the kingdom were delivered to him (D&C 110:11-16; 128:20-21) and were "never [to] be taken from [him] while [he was] in the world, neither in the world to come" (D&C 90:2-4). Thus, he holds the keys of this dispensation.

The keys committed to the foreordained prophet Joseph Smith included "the dispensation of the gospel of Abraham, saying that in us (the priesthood holders of this last dispensation) and our seed all generations after us should be blessed" (D&C 110:12). Earlier,[110] Joseph Smith had been told that he was from the loins of Abraham and that the promise of Abraham was Joseph's also because of this lineage. Therefore, he was to do the work of Abraham (D&C 132:30-32). Six months following the question and answer period where Joseph identified the rod and the root of Jesse (D&C 113:2-6), the Lord again revealed that Joseph Smith was the person through whom the covenant of Abraham would be fulfilled. "And as I said unto Abraham concerning the kindreds of the earth, even so I say unto my servant Joseph: In thee and in thy seed shall the kindred of the earth be blessed" (D&C 124:58). Further evidence of Joseph Smith's lineage being of Abraham is given later on in the same revelation cited above. Hyrum Smith, Joseph's older brother, is called to "the office of Priesthood and Patriarch, which was appointed unto him by his father, by blessing and also by right...[to] hold the keys of the patriarchal blessings upon the heads of all my people" (D&C 124:91-92). Joseph Smith, Sr., the father of Hyrum and Joseph Smith, Jr., was the first Patriarch to the Church. This office and keys were now to be held by Hyrum not only because of having been designated by his father but because it was his right as the oldest faithful living descendant of Abraham. As explained by the Prophet Joseph: "An Evangelist is a Patriarch, even the oldest man of the blood of Joseph or the seed of Abraham. Wherever the Church of Christ is established in the earth, there should be a Patriarch for the benefit of the posterity of the Saints, as it was with Jacob in giving his patriarchal blessing unto his sons, etc."[111] In the words of President Brigham Young, "[the Lord] has watched that family and that blood as it has circulated from its fountain to the birth of that man [Joseph Smith]" (JD 7:289-90).

---

[110] Although the reference cited is D&C 132, recorded July 12, 1843, it was revealed to Joseph Smith much earlier than this, as noted in the section heading.

[111] Teachings of the Prophet Joseph Smith, p. 151.

Descendants of Joseph and Ephraim

The covenant made to Abraham was passed on to Abraham's seed by birthright. Joseph, who was sold into Egypt, received the birthright (1 Chronicles 5:1-2). Many great covenants and blessings were likewise promised to Joseph and his seed (2 Nephi 3:4; 4:1-2). The fulfillment of Abraham's and Joseph's blessings were not limited to the Joseph Smith, Sr., family. Others of the lineage of Joseph were recipients of the same. At a conference of high priests 4 June 1833, John Johnson was given "a promise of eternal life inasmuch as he keepeth my commandments from henceforth—For he is a descendant of Joseph and a partaker of the blessings of the promise made unto his fathers—" (D&C 96:6-7).

On 1 August 1831, the residue of the elders of the Church were told they were to "push the people together from the ends of the earth. Wherefore,...let them preach the gospel in the regions round about" (D&C 58:44-46). The pushing of the people together from the ends of the earth was the blessing given by Moses to the seed of Joseph. Those pushed together were to be the ten thousands of Ephraim, and the thousands of Manasseh (Deuteronomy 33:13-17). Therefore the elders of the Church referred to above are the descendants of Joseph who are sent out to gather Ephraim and Manasseh from among the Gentiles. Nearly three months later (25 October 1831), the Lord reiterated this mission in a revelation to William E. McLellin (D&C 66:11). The Lord outlined the future events in the gathering of Israel to the promise lands of Jerusalem and Zion in Doctrine and Covenants 133. Those gathered or returning from the north countries (v. 26) are to "bring forth their rich treasures unto the children of Ephraim, my servants" (v. 30). The servants are those members of the Church who have already been gathered or pushed together in fulfillment of Joseph's blessing. Those coming from the north countries to the everlasting hills shall "be crowned with glory, even in Zion (the Americas), by the hands of the servants of the Lord, even the children of Ephraim" (v. 32). The Lord then confirmed that this will be the fulfillment of "the blessing of the everlasting God upon the tribes of Israel, and the richer blessing upon the head of Ephraim and his fellows" [others of Israel who have been gathered to Zion already or Gentiles who have been adopted into Israel] (v. 34). The Prophet Joseph further confirmed the servant concept in interpreting Isaiah's meaning of the phrase "Put on thy strength, O Zion—and what people had Isaiah reference to?" "He had reference to those whom God should call in the last days, who should hold the power of priesthood to bring again Zion, and the redemption of Israel; and to put on her strength is to put on the authority of the priesthood, *which she, Zion, has a right to by lineage*; also to return to that power which she had lost" (D&C 113:8; italics added). The Prophet also identified those in Zion as "the remnants of Israel in their scattered condition among the Gentiles" (v. 10). Ephraim was to fulfill the covenant of Abraham in gathering together Joseph's seed and others to the house of Israel in the latter days.

The Keys of Gathering

Moses appeared to Joseph Smith and Oliver Cowdery on 3 April 1836 in the newly built Kirtland Temple "and committed unto [them] the keys of the gathering of Israel from the four parts of the earth, and the leading of the ten tribes from the land of the north" (D&C 110:11).

The dedicatory prayer of the Kirtland Temple that was given by revelation to Joseph Smith further illustrates the servants' role in the gathering in the last days. The prayer asked that "[the Lord's] servants, the sons of Jacob, may gather out the righteous to build a holy city to [the Lord's] name" from all the nations of the earth (D&C 109:57-58). Although the Church members were called the sons of Jacob, it acknowledges that they were "identified with the Gentiles" (v. 60).[112] The prayer also asked that the children of Judah, the Lamanites, and "all the scattered remnants of Israel, who have been driven to the ends of the earth, come to a knowledge of the truth, believe in the Messiah, and be redeemed from oppression, and rejoice before thee" (vv. 62-67).

The Prophecies of Isaiah

The Savior declared to the Nephites that when the words of Isaiah "shall be fulfilled then is the fulfilling of the covenant which the father hath made unto his people, O house of Israel" (3 Nephi 20:12). He further commanded that the prophecies of Isaiah be searched because "he spake as touching all things concerning my people which are of the house of Israel; therefore it must needs be that he must speak also to the Gentiles" (3 Nephi 23:2).

Note that the Savior did not say that Isaiah spoke about the Gentiles, but that he was to speak "to the Gentiles." The reason Isaiah (through his writings) was to speak to the Gentiles is that the house

---

[112] President Wilford Woodruff referred to the Saints as Israelites, but Gentiles in a national capacity. "The Gospel is now restored to us Gentiles, for we are all Gentiles in a national capacity" (JD 18:220).

of Israel was scattered among them. If Isaiah were to speak all things concerning the house of Israel to them, he could not do so unless he spoke to the Gentiles among whom they were scattered. This is further confirmed by a subsequent verse in which the Savior declares that the words he was speaking to the Nephites should be written; then "according to the time and the will of the Father," they would "go forth unto the Gentiles" (3 Nephi 23:4).[113]

Jacob, son of Lehi, also said that "Isaiah spake concerning all the house of Israel" (2 Nephi 6:5). There are ten sections in the Doctrine and Covenants that quote or paraphrase Isaiah in the context of the Latter-day Saints being literal Israelites.

The Lord revealed anew the parable of the wheat and the tares and that its fulfillment would come in the latter days. As a lesson to be drawn from this parable, the Lord told the brethren that their priesthood had "continued through the lineage of [their] fathers—For [they were] lawful heirs, according to the flesh, and have been hid from the world with Christ in God," (D&C 86:1-9; compare Isaiah 49:2). Since these were first generation members of the Church, the fathers through whom this priesthood continued would not be their immediate fathers but as previously shown would logically refer to Abraham, Isaac, and Jacob, the covenant holders of past ages. This is further evidenced by the promise to Abraham that the priesthood would continue through the literal seed of his body (Abraham 2:11). The Lord continued the latter-day revelation with a declaration that his priesthood would continue through the lineage of these first-generation Church members "until the restoration of all things spoken by the mouths of all the holy prophets since the world began" (D&C 86:10). He promised further that if they continued in the Lord's goodness, they would be "a light unto the Gentiles, and through this priesthood, a savior unto [his] people Israel (v. 11). From these truths it can be discerned that the parable of the wheat and the tares teaches that the wheat pertains to the Israelites who are to be gathered from the tares who are the Gentiles. This interpretation is sustained by a later revelation:

> That the work of the gathering together of my saints may continue, that I may build them up unto my name upon holy places; for the time of harvest is come, and my word must needs be fulfilled.

---

[113] Nyman, Monte S. (1987). An Ensign To All People, Salt Lake City, Utah: Deseret Book Company, p. 39

Therefore, I must gather together my people according to the parable of the wheat and the tares, that the wheat may be secured in the garners to possess eternal life, and be crowned with celestial glory, when I shall come in the kingdom of my Father to reward every man according as his work shall be;

While the tares shall be bound in bundles, and their bands made strong, that they may be burned with unquenchable fire (D&C 101:64-66).

Joseph Smith understood that he was engaged in the second gathering of Israel prophesied by Isaiah (11:11). He marveled when he saw that Alvin would be in the celestial kingdom when "he had departed this life before the Lord had set his hand to gather Israel the second time, and had not been baptized for the remission of sins" (D&C 137:6).

In a revelation to Sidney Rigdon, the Lord commanded him to write for the Prophet Joseph that he might receive the scriptures "to the salvation of [the Lord's] elect; For they will hear my voice, and shall see me, and shall not be asleep, and shall abide the day of my coming; for they shall be purified, even as I am pure (D&C 35:20-21). The Lord then promised that Israel would be saved in his own due time (v. 25), verifying that his elect is Israel. This is reminiscent of Jesus' declaration: "My sheep hear my voice, and I know them, and they follow me" (John 10:27). Those with the blood of Israel respond to the gospel message because they were numbered with the house of Israel in the pre-mortal life and recognize these truths (see Deut. 32:8-9; Acts 17:26; Abr. 3:22-23; Alma 13:1-5).

A short time later the Lord revealed that the Church was to move to Ohio. From Ohio the Lord would send his representatives among all nations "for Israel shall be saved" (D&C 38:32-33). Three days after the above revelation the Lord promised James Covill that if he would be baptized he could participate in the covenant "to recover my people, which are of the house of Israel" (D&C 39:11). In June of 1831, the Lord referred to the saints as "my people, which are a remnant of Jacob, and those who are heirs according to the covenant" (D&C 52:2).

In D&C 45, the Lord revealed that the fulness of the gospel would come forth in the times of the Gentiles. "But they (the Gentiles) receive it not; for they perceive not the light" (vv. 28-29). Primarily those of the blood of Israel respond to the gospel messages. Joseph Smith also declared: "...but few of them will be gathered with the chosen family." (TPJS 15).

In speaking of the latter-day gathering to Zion, Isaiah said that the willing and obedient would eat the good of that land (Isaiah 1:19). That the Lord, through Isaiah, was speaking of latter-day Israel is confirmed by Oliver Cowdery's account of the angel Moroni's visit to Joseph Smith in September 1823. Oliver said, "Isaiah, who was on the earth at the time the ten tribes of Israel were led away captive from the land of Canaan, was shown not only their calamity and affliction, but the time when they were to be delivered." [114] In the same context, the Lord revealed the same concept and then warned that the rebellious would be cut off out of the land of Zion for "the rebellious are not of the blood of Ephraim" (D&C 64:34-36).

Other Israel References

The new song to be sung in Zion when it is established will declare that "the Lord hath redeemed his people, Israel" (D&C 84:98-100). He declared that he had much people in the area of New York and the regions round about (D&C 100:3). He spoke also of Salem, Massachusetts (D&C 111:2). Much people can refer only to Israel since he wasn't speaking of total population. In speaking of the future establishment of the city of Zion (New Jerusalem), he referred to the time when the army of Israel would become very great (D&C 105:26-27, 30-31). He referred to his bishops as judges in Israel (D&C 107:72).

In crossing the plains, Brigham Young received a revelation regarding the organization of the people into companies. The Lord referred to the Camp of Israel (D&C 136:1), and compared them to the children of Israel coming out of Egypt (v. 22).

Conclusion

Following the First Vision, the prophet Joseph Smith was visited by various angels to restore their keys, power, and authority to gather Israel from among the Gentiles and from their being scattered upon all the face of the earth. The members of The Church of Jesus Christ of Latter-day Saints are those Israelites who have already been gathered. However, there yet remain millions more to be gathered. This gathering when completed will far exceed the previous gatherings of Israel in other dispensations. Not only will it include the thousands of Manasseh and the tens of thousands of Ephraim but will include millions of Lamanites,

---

[114] Cowdery, Oliver, <u>Messenger and Advocate</u>, April, 1835. pp. 109-110.

Jews, and descendants of the ten lost tribes of Israel. The members of the restored church of Jesus Christ are the literal seed of Abraham and of Israel who will be the Lord's servants to establish Israel as the kingdom of God, and Zion as the New Jerusalem, and usher in the millennial reign of the Lord Jesus Christ. To these great truths the Doctrine and Covenants as revelation to the apostles and prophets of the latter days bears repeated witness.

Doctrine and Covenants Revelations Concerning Literal Israel

	Section and Verses	Annotated Confirmation
1.	27:10	The promises to Abraham, Isaac, and Jacob remain
2.	35:20-21, 25	The elect (covenant people) will hear of his voice and be saved
3.	38:33	Israel saved from all nations
4.	39:11	Covenant to recover the house of Israel
5.	45:17, 28-29	The restoration of scattered Israel among the Gentiles—few Gentiles join
6.	52:2	The Church a remnant of Jacob—heirs to the covenant
7.	58:44-46 (65:1)	Push the people together from the ends of the earth
8.	64:36	The rebellious not of Ephraim
9.	84:6-34, 99-100	Priesthood holders of Abraham, the Lord redeems Israel
10.	86:1-11 (esp.8-11)	Wheat and tares, Israel hidden among the Gentiles
11.	96:6-7	Descendants of Joseph
12.	98:16	Turn the hearts of (Abraham's) children to their fathers
13.	100:3	Much people (Israel) in this place
14.	101:64-65	Wheat and tares (Israel among the Gentiles)
15.	103:15-19	Ye are of Israel and Abraham
16.	105:26-27, 30-31	Army of Israel to become great
17.	107:72	Judges in Israel
18.	109:58, 60, 67	Sons of Jacob to gather out righteous among the Gentiles
19.	110:11-12	Keys of the gathering and dispensation of the gospel of Abraham

20.	111:2	Many people (Israel) in this city
21.	113:2-10	Joseph Smith—descendant of Judah and Joseph
22.	124:1, 58, 91-92	Joseph Smith—fulfills covenant of Abraham, patriarchal lineage
23.	132:30-31	Joseph Smith—the seed of Abraham
24.	133:12, 30, 32, 34	Ephraim the servants of the Lord
25.	136:1, 22	Camps of Israel led as the children of Israel
26.	137:6	Gather Israel the second time

Bibliography

1. Benson, Ezra Taft. A Witness and A Warning Deseret Book, Salt Lake City, 1988.
2. Cowdery, Oliver. Message and Advocate April 1835.
3. Journal of Discourses, 26 volumes.
4. McConkie, Bruce R. Doctrines of Salvation Bookcraft, 1956.
5. McConkie, Bruce R. A New Witness for the Articles of Faith Deseret Book, 1985.
6. Nelson, Russell M. BYU Devotional Address. Publication pending.
7. Nyman, Monte S. An Ensign to All People Deseret Book, 1987.
8. Smith, Joseph F. Gospel Doctrine Deseret Book, Salt Lake City, 11th edition, 1959.
9. Smith, Joseph Fielding. Teachings of the Prophet Joseph Smith Deseret Book, Salt Lake City, 1974.

Appendix 2
The Lifted Ensign—A Call to Israel

An original dramatic poem, written especially for the occasion of General Conference, April 1930 by Elder Orson F. Whitney.

> "And he shall set up an ensign
> for the nations, and shall assemble
> the outcasts of Israel, and gather to-
> gether the dispersed of Judah from
> the four corners of the earth."
> Isaiah 11:12.

Characters Impersonated:
ELIAS :: EPHRAIM :: JUDAH

ELIAS:
A voice that crieth in the Wilderness:
"Make plain and straight the Highway of our God!"
One Hundred Years, on Time's swift pinions flown,
Since raised the Ensign for the Gathering—
One hundred years, and still the standard waves,
Summoning the chosen from world-wandering,
Calling the covenant people from afar,
To greet the coming of their God and King.

Children of Jacob, Isaac, Abraham,
Sheep of the flock the Shepherd comes to fold!
How have ye answered to his beckoning call?
What have ye done his pathway to prepare?
Heber J. Grant, Conference Report, April 1930, p.34[115]

---

[115] Orson F. Whitney, General Conference, April 1930, pages 33-41

Give answer, Ephraim, from thy mountain height,
Where streams the signal seen and sung of yore—
First-born of God in these, Earth's final days,
Speak thou, and let the winds thy story tell!

EPHRAIM:

I hear thee, and with joy I answer thee:
'Twas mine to welcome the return of Truth,
Of old from Error's wide domain withdrawn;
Mine to unshroud the buried mystery
Of mighty nations, whispering from the dust;
Mine to unfurl the Ensign, and to sound
O'er sea and land the tidings wonderful;
Flooding the world with truth and righteousness,
Thrusting the sickle in the golden grain,
Reaping a ripened field, and garnering
The earliest sheaves of Israel's harvest home.

I've toiled and wept and bled to bring once more
The fulness of Christ's Message unto men;
To build redemptive Temples, that the dead,
Obedient to law in spirit realms,
Might with the living share in joys divine.
More wouldst thou hear?—
There's more I fain would tell.

ELIAS

Tell on!—tell on! Truth wearies not mine ear.

EPHRAIM:

Expelled by tyranny from Freedom's ground,
I tracked the lone untrodden wilderness.
Here 'neath my virile touch, once barren wilds
Now sing for joy and bloom delightsomely.
I've planted Zion's outposts, firm and strong,
Rock-fortressed by the everlasting hills,
Where Faith expectantly doth bide the hour
When Zion's self from Eden's soil shall rise,

Thrilled by the glad acclaim: "The Bridegroom comes!"
Nor all my ministries on Western shores,
Nor all my sympathies with next of kin.
Have I not stood on ancient Olivet,
And offered prayer to heaven for Judah's weal?
Have I not combed the universe and drawn
The choice of nations to this favored land,
Where homing tribes shall shout to trembling hills,
And lift hosannas to the listening skies
That light the towers of New Jerusalem?

By these and kindred works my faith is shown.
Thus have I answered to the Shepherd's call.

ELIAS:

And answered well. And He whose day now dawns
Shall crown thy valor with a recompense
As boundless, endless as eternity.
Now, Judah, tell thy tale! What deeds of thine
Are strewn as flowers along Messiah's way?

JUDAH:

Messiah?—Him I see not in the man
Whom Christians name the Christ, their holy one.
I see not in their God my fathers' God,
Whose covenant abides with Abraham:
Who spake to Moses in the fiery Mount,
And gave the Law to govern Israel.
Blind am I to what Ephraim beholds.
Perchance the air is purer, view more large,
On yonder height where stalwartly he stands,
Than in the misty vale where I respire.
Thinkst thou I err, his thought interpreting?

But I am with him in the war for right,
For justice and the freedom of the world.
And to this cause give I a willing hand,
And pledge my friendship, faith and loyalty.

ELIAS:

Thou sayest well—yet well might'st say far more
For Israel's God, Jehovah, Lord of All,
Who gave the Gospel as He gave the Law,
And died that endless death might vanquished be.
What limit to His merit or His claim?

JUDAH:

Plead not with me my ancient faith to change—
Older than aught by Christians deemed divine;
Pure as the snowy peaks of Lebanon,
That pour reviving streams o'er thirsty plains.
What nobler doctrine than the Decalogue?
What higher law than Justice can'st thou name?

ELIAS:

Is Justice more than Mercy—more than Love?
No need to change thy faith, but build thereon.
If thou the Perfect Law wouldst comprehend,
Its loftiest, purest, heavenmost height attain,
Add unto justice the pure love of God—
Sweet Charity, of graces all the crown.

JUDAH:

Justice—not Mercy—is the Jew's demand.
And tell me, when did Christian charity
Mean justice for the wronged, down-trodden Jew?
Mercy, forsooth! what mercy have they shown,
Who slaughter 'neath the banner of the Cross?
Too much we hear of love and charity,
From lips of hate, from hearts of cruelty,
Boasting a leader whom they follow not,
Prating of love, but never practising.
This Jesus, whom they laud, not emulate,
Good man—e'en great perchance. But why a God?
Joseph and Mary's son, a common Jew,
Who sat at feet of rabbis famed for lore,

And learned from them, yet brought forth nothing new.
Why should the knee of Israel bend to him?

ELIAS:

Sat He at no man's feet for power to save
And lift up fallen worlds. His wisdom came
From heights more distant than the unseen stars,
Fresh as the morning dew upon the flower;
Pure as the snow—so white on Lebanon
Till tainted by the soil through which it flows—
Truth by tradition's muddy stream unroiled.

The sapient rabbis, famed for antique lore,
Might well have learned from Him—but would not learn.
The wisest of the scribes and pharisees,
Astounded, routed were, and put to shame
By One who spake as no man since or ere.

Old was his doctrine—truth is ever old—
Old as its parent spring, Eternity,
Old upon earth, from Adam until now.
Yet seemed it new to them;—and this the cause,
The chief and primal cause of that great crime
Which on the cross He pardoned and forgave.

Man—merest man will die a friend to save.
Who but a God, to save both foe and friend?
And very God was He, though human-born,
Divinely-gotten Child of Deity.

But why waste words upon those recreant Jews,
Those pseudo Christians—false that mask as true?
The salt can lose its savor—so with them—
Unworthy parts, bespeaking not the whole.
Why dwell upon these human happenings?
Lift thought and argument to higher planes.

JUDAH:

Amen! say I. And now to me make plain—

To me, who am so dull—this mystery:
What need had Israel of this Nazarene?
Why came a Christ, great Moses having come?
And why a Gospel when the Law was known?

ELIAS:

What need of Christ—the Lord—since Moses came?
Moses to Christ was but as part to whole,
Preface to book, mere river to the sea,
And all the dispensations of the past,
When heaven hath gladdened earth with spirit showers,
Are but as streams that to one Ocean flow.

Why separate the Gospel from the Law—
Greater and less—container and contained?
Why part God from his prophet messengers,
Sent from Above to voice and work his will,
And preparation make for mightier things
Than e'er were known among the sons of men;
Completing what creation's morn began,
When Gods in glory launched a universe?

JUDAH:

But Abraham—the solemn Covenant—
Jehovah's sacred promise to His own:
"In thee and thine all men, all nations blest"—
Spoken these words upon the idle wind,
That now they be as though they ne'er had been?

ELIAS:

'Twas Christ made covenant with Abraham,
Jesus, Jehovah—for the twain are one;—
Then gave Himself that covenant to fulfill:
And mixt His people with earth's alien tribes,
That all—not Israel only—might be blest,
Nor least and last of nations fail to share
In blessings showered through him upon the world,
Sprinkled, as rain, with his believing blood;

Peopling the arid wastes of unbelief
With souls responsive to the clarion call
Shaking the seas and isles and continents,
And gathering what was scattered ages gone.

JUDAH:

But Moses—what of him? Lived he for naught?
Sayest thou his mighty mission was in vain?

ELIAS:

Nay; but to round his glorious ministry,
And link the lesser with the greater part,
Making effectual all that went before,
In this, the dispensation last of all,
Came he the Keys of Gathering to restore;
Lest Ephraim's rallying standard wave in vain
O'er Joseph's land and Zion's, known of old
By seers and prophets from thy household sprung,
Whose sacred words flow down the centuries
To find fulfillment in this ample age,
Where past and present, sire and son must join,
Perfection reign, and all in Christ be one.

Ephraim his part hath played, and thou no less,
In God's great drama—"Marvel and Wonder" named.
Wherefore, complete thy story, well begun.
What hast thou done His pathway to prepare?

JUDAH:

His pathway!—his, the peasant carpenter,
Whose body, stolen from the tomb, long since
Hath crumbled and returned to native dust?
Granting, for argument, he is to come,
Why should I strew with palms his earthward way?
Why for his coming should my soul prepare?

ELIAS:

Because He is thy Father and thy Friend,
Because He is the God of Israel—
Buried yet risen Savior of mankind,
Author and Giver of the life divine.
What hast thou done that He on earth may reign?

Silent? Then wouldst thou choose one speak for thee,
Who ne'er unfriendly was to thee or thine,
But sympathetic in thy sorrows all?
For thou hast borne the brunt of martyrdom,
Alike in Christian and in heathen lands,
Enduring long and suffering patiently,
While lesser breeds have trampled thee and spurned.
Driven—despoiled—tortured and trodden down,
Drinking the bitter cup, Captivity,
Yet still, through groaning, pain-racked centuries
Honoring Jehovah's name, Jehovah's law,
Spreading the knowledge of the living God
Amid the shrines of Baal and Ashtoreth.

Why 'twas thy hand the instrument became
Of purpose heaven-ordained ere earth began,
Whereby, through sacrifice and death, came Life,
To rescue and redeem a fallen world,—
No mortal knoweth. Only this men know:
Christ did not cast thee off. He that forgave
Is still thy Friend—as are true Christians all;
For none love God who hate what God doth love.

Forth in these modern days thine eager hand,
To build anew the old Jerusalem,
To raise once more her walls, oft leveled down;
To gather in thy sons and daughters fair,
And sow a sterile land with fruitfulness;
Redeeming thus thine ancient heritage,
That Zion's King may sit on David's throne.
Not all thy sons thy wearied arms uphold,
Not all are Hurs and Aarons in the strife.
Summon thy worldings from the tinseled show,

Where folly reigns and ruin works its will.
Teach them to play a better, nobler part,
And walk with thee the greater "Great White Way."

Rouse all that slumber beneath sordid spells,
Or unto gods of dust low homage pay;
Bid them to bring their gold and jewels rare,
Their heaped up stores of precious merchandise,
Their wealth, like Pelion on Ossa piled,
And beautify the Holy Place of Him
Whose law shall yet from Zion's land go forth,
Whose royal edict from Jerusalem.
For Israel o'er Amalek must prevail,
And repossess in full the Promised Land.

Ah! Judah, couldst thou see what Ephraim sees—
Thy monarch in that lowly Nazarene,
Long-symboled by the oft-slain paschal lamb,
Prophetic of the Sacrifice Supreme.

Would thou couldst see what ancient seers discerned,
What spirit-quickened eyes may now behold—
Messiah in that Prophet first-of-all,
The Moses of a mightier Exodus
Than e'er was dreamt of in rabbinic lore;
Deliverer of a captive universe,
In bondage to the powers of death and hell!

And thy Deliverer in a day to come,
When hostile legions thunder at thy gates,
When half thy city hath become a spoil,
As written in the scroll of prophecy.
Then shalt thou see and feel His wounded hands,
Then shalt thou fall and worship at His feet;
And all that fight 'gainst Jacob's, Judah's God,
Shall be as dust and ashes whirl-wind-blown,
As flying chaff before the hurricane.

JUDAH:

What confirmation hath this mighty claim?

How can I know if such great things be true?
If I be blind, who will my sight unscale?

ELIAS:

He who makes blind to see and deaf to hear!—
Hearken to Him and whoso'er He sends.
Bow to the sceptre of the Son of God,
The Gospel of the High and Holy One,
And by that Gift which maketh manifest
Thou'lt clearly see and of a surety know
The message Ephraim brings thee is divine,—
Old and yet new, the Everlasting Truth,
Pure from the presence of our fathers' God.
Fresh from the fountains of Eternity.

JUDAH:

Why Ephraim? Why his proud pre-eminence,
Towering amid the tents of Israel?
Why should his word or thine determine all?

ELIAS:

Because it is the word of Israel's God,
Whose servant I, as I would fain be thine;—
The God of Moses and of Abraham,
The God of patriarchs and prophets all,
The God of Israel free and Israel chained;
God of the humble and the pure-in-heart;
God of the just, in every age and clime;
The Christ of Bethlehem and Calvary,
The King of Kings, the crucified and crowned.
Come, weary-laden, He will give thee rest,
And thou shalt tread the rose-strewn path of peace.

EPHRAIM:

Heed, Judah! heed Messiah's messenger,
Hearken to me, thy brother and thy friend.
No more doth envy of thee sour my soul,

Nor doth thine anger vex me, as of yore.
Forgiven as I forgive, clean, clear I stand,
And I am sent Good Tidings to proclaim.
No man-made creed—no dogma vague, unsound—
The Ancient Faith, pure, simple, sweet, sublime,
The Gospel in its plentitude of power,
The Gospel in its fulness—this I bring.

ELIAS:

Judah! 'tis Ephraim calls—he loves thee well,
His hand extends, his heart, to welcome thee.
Why stand aloof? Why doubt and hesitate?
Jerusalem and Zion are as one.
See Japheth launch his ships to people them!
The Gentile, all unknowingly doth serve
The cause of Him who summons Israel
To Joseph's land, to Judah's hills and vales.
Behold them in their flight from Babel's doom,
Borne on the shoulders of the Philistine?

Be not outstript in such a glorious race.
Judah, arise! Put on thine ancient might,
Expand thy soul, enlarge thy sympathy;
Join hands with Ephraim, and bring to pass
All that the prophets and the seers foretold!

JUDAH:

Thy speech I can believe most kindly meant,
Thy motive pure and generous and just.
But who can change the course of destiny?
Who void what Great Jehovah hath decreed?
'Tis conscience guides me, and high Heaven alone
Doth hold, of that mysterious lock, the key.

Yet something tells me we shall meet again.
God grant it be as friends! And so, farewell.

131

Index to Ephraim:
Chosen of the Lord

A

Aaronic Priesthood, 112
Abraham, 8, 17, 24, 26, 27, 33, 37, 39
  covenant of, 111-13
Adam, 112
Adam-ondi-Ahman, 103
Adoption, 13, 18, 33, 38, 63
Adversary. See Satan
Ahaz, 31, 55
America, 22, 23, 46, 52, 53, 79
Ammi, 40, 41
Amos, 35
Angels, 35
Apostasy, 33-34, 55-56
Apostles, 59
Armor of God, 74-75
Arzareth, 31
Asenath, 17
Assyria, 29, 30, 31, 33, 34, 35, 38,
  44, 47, 52, 54, 55, 63

B

Baal, 30, 41
Babylonians, 54
Ballard, Melvin J., on the chosen
  people, 10
  on Ephraim's responsibility, 2-3
  on example, 99-100
  on the gathering, 80, 89
  on a peculiar people, 98
  on privileges of Ephraim, 105
  on resources for Ephraim, 79
Baptism, 38, 62
Benjamin, 26, 46

Benson, Ezra Taft, on a chosen
  generation, 13-14
Bethel, 26, 27
Bethlehem, 46
Bible, 45, 60
Birthright, 22, 24, 114
Blood of Ephraim, 62, 63
Book of Mormon, coming forth of
  the, 38-39
  Ephraim in the, 51-58
  Joseph Smith translates the, 112
  judgment from the, 57, 58
  on the New Jerusalem, 88
  as the stick of Ephraim, 45, 51-52

C

Caleb, 23
Camp of Israel, 118
Canaan, 18, 19, 20, 22-23, 25, 34, 46
Carthage, Ill., 67
Celestial kingdom, 117
Character, 98
Confusion, 7
Conversion, 40
Couple missionaries, 72-73
Covenants, 39, 43, 44, 46-47, 47, 53,
  54, 83, 111-13, 116
Covill, James, 117
Cowdery, Oliver, 40, 41, 46, 90, 94,
  115, 118
Cush, 38

D

Dark ages, 43
David, 42, 112

Dead, work for the, 86-87, 105-6
Despair, 73
Devil. See Satan
Doctrine and Covenants, 114, 116, 119-20
  Ephraim in the, 59-68
Doom, 37
Dreams, 19-20, 26
Dyer, Alvin R., on those who accept the gospel, 84

E
Ebal, Mount, 27
Egypt, Ephraim calls to, 34
  Israel called out of, 44
  Israel came out of, 23
  Israel in, 22
  Israel to be gathered from, 38
  Jacob in, 20
  Jesus Christ in, 44
  Joseph sold into, 17, 114
  Moses in, 30
  Moses lead Israel out of, 35
Elam, 38
Elders, 24, 77-78
Elias, 4, 112
Endowments, 67, 95
Enlightenment, 43
Enoch, 107
Environment, 100-104
Ephod, 33
Ephraim, to be gathered first, 81-84
  to be redeemed, 44-45
  blankets the earth with missionaries, 78-80
  blessings of, 2-5, 14, 18-22, 91-95, 105
  blood of, 62, 63
  in The Book of Mormon, 51-58
  and the building of New Jerusalem, 87-91
  as a chosen people, 7-15, 104-9
  city of, 26
  day of, 104
  descendants of, 114-15
  in the Doctrine and Covenants, 59-68

  does not have rebellious blood, 61-63
  elders of Church are largely of, 24
  entered an alliance, 55
  faithfulness of, 71-73
  to find the lost sheep, 77-84
  foreordination of, 7-15, 24
  to gather at Adam-ondi-Ahman, 103
  gathering of, 81-84
  and God's judgments, 29-35
  has spirit of adventure, 104
  Hosea's prophecies of, 37-38
  is fulfilling the fulness of the Gentiles, 21
  in Jackson County, 66-67
  Jacob's blessing upon, 18-22
  Joseph Smith purely of, 65, 81
  and Judah, 55, 100
  as a judge, 64
  keys are with, 92
  land of, 25-28
  mission of, 3-4
  mixed among the Gentiles, 34
  Moses blesses, 23
  Mount, 46
  naming of, 18
  opposed in the Latter-days, 69-75
  and the other tribes, 80-81
  and the perfecting of the Saints, 97-109
  promises to, 52-53
  prophecies of gathering of, 37-48
  recognizes truth, 101
  resources provided for, 78-79
  responsibility of, 2-5, 12-14
  and the return of the tenth, 47-49
  scattering of, 29-35
  as the second son of Joseph, 17
  stick of, 45, 59-61
  and temple work, 85-95
  treasures unto, 66-68
  was leading northern tribe, 26
  as the watchman, 106
  wickedness of, 33-34
Esau, 17, 22
Euphrates River, 31
Exaltation, 85

Example, 99-100
Ezekiel, on the gathering, 45

F
Families, mixed tribes in, 83
Fear, 73
First Vision, 118
Foreordination, 8-15, 24, 71, 79, 87,
  103-4, 106, 113
Forgiveness, 61

G
Gathering of Israel, 21, 24, 29, 34,
  38-49, 54, 55, 56, 57-58, 62,
  77-84, 88, 89, 100, 117-18
  keys of, 115, 118
Genealogy, 67
Gentiles, to be numbered with Israel,
  40, 41-42, 82-83
  do not perceive light, 117
  Ephraim is mixed among the, 34
  fulness of the, 21, 39
  gathering of Ephraim from the, 54
  gathering of the, 82-83, 115, 118
  given opportunity to accept the
    gospel, 24
  Israel gathered from the, 62
  Israel scattered among the, 32, 38,
    77, 115
  nature of the, 99-100
  purging the blood of the, 63
  Samaritans married, 27
Geography, 25-28
Gerizim, Mount, 27
Gloom, 73
Gomer, 29, 37
Grant, Heber J., 4

H
Hagar, 17
Hamath, 38
Hauns Mill, Mo., 67
Heavenly Father, remembers his
  chosen people, 80-81
Herod, 44, 46
Holy Ghost, 38, 63, 79, 102
Hope, 37
Hosea, Jesus Christ quoted, 43

as prophet of Ephraim, 35, 37-38,
  40, 45
symbolic marriages of, 29-30
Hyde, Orson, 90

I
Idolatry, 26-27, 33, 41, 45
Influence, 98-99
Isaac, 17, 39
Isaiah, on The Book of Mormon, 53-54
  on the gathering, 40
  on gathering Ephraim, 47
  preached in Northern Kingdom, 54
  prophecies of, 21, 115-18
  on the Second Coming, 54
  "their works are in the dark," 7
  understanding, 25
  warned Israel, 29, 35
  warned Judah, 55
  on watchman, 106
Ishmael, 17, 51, 52
Israel, counting of tribes of, 18-19
  division of, 26-28
  gathering of, 21, 24, 29, 34, 38-49,
    54, 55, 56, 57-58, 62,
    77-84, 88, 89, 100, 115, 117-18
  literal, 119-20
  lost tribe of, 3-4, 31, 32, 56, 66,
    90-94, 119
  Moses blesses, 22-24
  scattering of, 13, 24, 29-35, 37-49,
    52, 55, 57-58, 66

J
Jackson County, Mo., 66-67, 87, 88, 89
Jacob (Bible patriarch), at Bethel, 26
  blesses Ephraim, 18-22
  covenant with, 44
  gathering of the remnants of, 39
  gave patriarchal blessings, 113
  given America, 53
  name of, 17, 20-21
  Rachel was favored wife of, 65
  sons of, 115
  tribes of, 41
  was given the birthright, 22
  wrestles an angel, 34-35

135

Jacob (son of Lehi), 116
Jeremiah, on the gathering, 39-40, 46
  on the Gentiles, 41, 42
  on lost tribes, 94
  on the scattering, 35
Jeroboam, 26, 27
Jerusalem, 26, 27, 51, 55, 94
Jesse, 57, 112, 113
Jesus Christ, atonement of, 30
  David is symbolic of, 42
  in Egypt, 44
  gospel of, 62
  and Herod's slaying of children, 46
  on his sheep, 32, 117
  in the land of Ephraim, 26, 27-28
  light of, 56
  on the perfecting process, 97
  preparing for the coming of, 12, 15
  quotes Hosea, 43
  resurrection of, 43
  scattered Israel had no leadership
    from, 33
  second coming of, 12, 15, 54, 66,
    67, 69, 74, 99, 103, 106, 107-8
Jews, 27, 94
Jezreel, 29, 38
Joel, 35
Johnson, John, 114
John the Revelator, 81
Jonah, 35
Jordan River, 26
Joseph (Bible patriarch), America
  given to house of, 46
  blessed Israel in Egypt, 22
  descendants of, 114-15
  dream of, 19-20
  Ephraim is a descendant of, 65
  as a fruitful bough, 51-53
  is not counted as a tribe, 18-19
  Jacob's blessing upon, 18-22
  Joseph Smith is a descendant of,
    65, 112
  lineage of, 2, 17
  Moses blesses people of, 23
  naming of the sons of, 18
  promises to, 52-53
  stick of, 60
  was buried in Shechem, 27

Joseph (son of Lehi), 60
Joshua, 22, 23, 25, 27
Judah, Ahaz of, 31, 55
  to be gathered, 38, 58, 94, 115
  Caleb was of, 23
  and Ephraim, 56, 100
  faithfulness of, 44
  Isaiah warned, 54
  Jesse of, 112
  Joseph Smith is a descendant of, 65
  poem about, 4
  restoration of, 46
  stick of, 45, 60
Judgment, 29-35, 57, 58, 64

K
Keys, of the gathering, 115, 118
  priesthood, 92, 112, 113
Kimball, Heber C., 90
Kimball, Spencer W., on preparation,
  71, 72
  on the scattering of Israel, 32
Kirtland, Ohio, 61, 90
Kirtland Temple, 94, 112

L
Lamanites, 68, 88, 90, 92, 115,
  118-19
Last days, 20, 42
Law of Moses, 27
Lehi, 25, 51
  on The Book of Mormon, 61
Levi, 19
Liberty Jail, Mo., 67
"Lifted Ensign-A Call to Israel is,
  The" (poem), 2, 4-5, 121-31
Lineage, and adoption, 12-13
  declaration of, 1
  of Ephraim, 104
  of Joseph, 2
  of Judah, 112
Lo-ammi, 30
Lo-ruhamah, 29
Lost sheep, gathering of, 77-84
Lost tribes of Israel, 3-4, 31, 32, 56,
  66, 90-94, 119
Loyalty, 73
Lucifer. <u>See</u> Satan

M

Machir, 22

Man, nature of, 7

Manasseh, 17, 18, 21, 22, 24, 25, 51, 52-53, 81, 104, 114

Matthew, quotes Jeremiah, 46

Maxwell, Neal A., on attitude of superiority, 101-2

McConkie, Bruce R., on stick of Joseph, 60

McKay, David O., on radiation of character, 98

McLellin, William E., 114

Melchizedek Priesthood, 112

Mercy, 40

Micah, 35

Michael, 69

Missionary work, 3-4, 40, 58, 71-73, 77-84

Missouri, 63, 66-67, 87, 88, 89, 111

Moroni, 21, 38, 40, 41-42, 46, 59-60, 112-13, 118

Moses, appeared to Joseph Smith, 115

  blesses Ephraim, 18

  blesses Israel, 22-24

  gives blessing, 114

  had priesthood, 112

  Jehovah promised, 30

  law of, 27

  lead Israel out of Egypt, 35, 39, 44, 111-12

  supported by Levites, 19

Mount Ebal, 27

Mount Gerizim, 27

Mount Sinai, 19

N

Names, Biblical, 17-18

Nephi, on The Book of Mormon, 38

  on Isaiah, 21, 25, 37, 46

  "I will go and do," 73

Nephites, 97, 115

New Jerusalem, 27, 53, 87-91, 112, 118

Nicodemus, 85

"Noble and great ones," 8-10, 106

Numbers, Book of, 25

Nyman, Monte S., "The Second Gathering of the Literal Seed," 2, 111-20

O

Ohio, 117

Ordinances, 38, 85

P

Palestine, 94

Pathros, 38

Patriarchal blessings, 1, 34, 104, 113

Paul, on the armor of God, 74

  on doers of the word, 63

  on foreordination, 8-9, 10

  on the Gentiles, 38, 41

  on rebellious Israel, 62

  on the spirit of fear, 73

Pearl of Great Price, 60, 111

Pekah, 55

Penrose, Charles W., on Ephraim's recognition of truth, 101

Perfecting the Saints, 97-109

Peterson, H. Burke, on a royal generation, 103

Pharisees, 43

Philistines, 26

Plan of Salvation, 56

Pratt, Harold W., on the other tribes, 80

Pratt, Orson, on the blessings of Ephraim, 14

  on the symbol of two records, 60

Preaching the gospel. See Missionary work

Premortal life, 8-15, 24, 32, 69, 71, 81, 83, 101-2, 103-4, 106, 107, 113, 117

Preparation, 12, 15, 66, 69, 71, 72

Priesthood, 33, 38, 112, 114-15, 116

Prophecies, of gathering, 37-48

Prophets, 35, 59, 71

Psalms, on Ephraim, 48

R

Rachel, 46, 65

Rebekah, 17

Reformation, 43
Rehoboam, 26
Remaliah, 55
Renaissance, 43
Repentance, 45
Restoration, 32-33, 38, 42, 45, 46, 55, 56
Resurrection, 43, 44-45
Reuben, 18, 22
Revelation, 41, 88, 112, 116
Rezin, 55
Richards, LeGrand, on the gathering, 100-101
  on Rocky Mountain prophecy, 46
Rigdon, Sidney, 117
Rocky Mountains, 46, 89-90
Rome, 62
Ruhamah, 40, 41

S
Sacrament, 59
Samaritans, 27-28
Satan, fights against Ephraim, 69-70
  fights against missionaries, 71-73
  fights against the youth, 72
  increase in power of, 73-75
  opposition of, 27
  uses discord and divisiveness, 102
Scattering of Israel, 13, 24, 29-35, 37-49, 52, 55, 57-58, 66
Sealings, 67, 94
Second Coming, 54, 67, 74, 99, 103, 106, 107-8
  preparation for the, 12, 15, 66, 69
Selfishness, 106
Shechem, 26, 27
Sheep analogy, 32, 77-84, 117
Shiloh, 26, 27
Shinar, 38
Simeon, 18
Sinai, Mount, 19
Smith, Alvin, 117
Smith, Hyrum, 113
Smith, Hyrum G., on blessing of Ephraim, 105
  on Ephraim's responsibility, 2
  on loyalty, 73
  on patriarchal blessings, 104

on temple blessings, 92-93
Smith, Joseph, Jr., on the armor of God, 74
  on confusion of the world, 7
  on the covenant restored, 47
  as a descendant of Joseph, 112
  as a descendant of Joseph and Judah, 65
  engaged in second gathering, 117
  first vision of, 118
  on foreordination, 11-12
  foreordination concept revealed to, 15
  on freeing the prisoners, 84
  fulfills Abraham's covenant, 112-13
  on the fulness of the Gentiles, 39
  on the gathering, 81
  on the Gentiles, 117
  "Go Forward," 108-9
  had the Spirit, 58
  made one change to Hosea, 44
  Moroni's instructions to, 21, 38, 40, 41-42, 46, 59-60, 112-13, 118
  on perfecting the Saints, 97
  as a pure Ephraimite, 65, 81
  on purging the old blood, 63
  received keys, 94
  Rocky Mountain prophecy of, 89-90
  on the sacrament, 59
  on Satan, 69
  on Satan's opposition, 26-27
  as the stem of Jesse, 56-57, 65
  and the stick of Ephraim, 60
  on work for the dead, 105-6
Smith, Joseph, Sr., 113, 114
Smith, Joseph F., on being one, 102
  on the blood of Ephraim, 47
Smith, Joseph Fielding, on benefits of the gospel, 98-99
  on Ephraim, 67-68
  on Ephraim in Zion, 103
  on Ephraim's keys, 92
  on Ephraim's temple building, 87, 94
  on foreordination, 9
  on the gathering, 81
  on leadership from Ephraim, 105
  on lineage, 12-13
  on lost tribes, 93

on mortals performing ordinances,
85-86
on the New Jerusalem, 88
on our special call, 74
on patriarchal blessings, 104
Snow, Erastus, on the chosen
spirits, 8
on hunting for the Elders, 77-78
on the record of Ephraim, 51-52
on work for the dead, 86-87
Solomon, 26
Sychar, 27
Syria, 31, 35, 55

T
Tabernacle, 19, 27
Temple work, 85-95
Temptations, 71, 74
Teraphim, 33
Trials, 74

U
Unicorns, symbol of, 23-24

V
Visions, 35

W
Wells, Rulon S., on the gathering, 85
on natural selection, 106
on resources for Ephraim, 79
on work for the dead, 87
Whitney, Orson F., on a chosen
people, 12
on Ephraim's responsibility, 3
on the gathering, 84
"Lifted Ensign-A Call to Israel is,
The," 2, 4-5, 121-31
on lost tribes, 93-94
Woodruff, Wilford, on becoming a
Zion people, 108
on a chosen people, 11
on the lost tribes, 91
on preparing and gathering, 81-82
on Rocky Mountain prophecy, 89-90

Y
Young, Brigham, on the gathering, 81
on gathering the Gentiles, 82-83
on Joseph Smith, 113
on Joseph Smith as a pure
Ephraimite, 65n, 81
on location of Ephraim, 78
on the New Jerusalem, 87-88
on perfection of the Saints, 99
received revelation of Camp of
Israel, 118
on searching for other tribes, 77
on spirit of adventure, 104
on trials, 70-71
Wilford Woodruff on, 90
Youth, 72

Z
Zechariah, on the gathering, 48-49
Zenos, 48
Zion, 103, 111, 114
Zion's Camp, 90